Total Body Workout

Katerina Spilio & Erica Gordon-Mallin

hinkler

Published by Hinkler Books Pty Ltd 2017
45–55 Fairchild Street
Heatherton Victoria 3202 Australia
www.hinkler.com

hinkler

Copyright © Hinkler Books Pty Ltd 2014

Created by Moseley Road Inc.
President: Sean Moore
General Manager: Karen Prince
Editor: Jo Weeks
Designer: Tina Vaughan

Photographer: FineArtsPhotoGroup.com
Models: Joseph Benedict, Jillian Langenau
Illustrator: Hector Aiza/3DLabz
Prepress: Splitting Image

ISBN: 978 1 4889 3436 0

Printed and bound in China

Always do the warm-up exercises before attempting any individual exercises. It is recommended that you check with
your doctor or healthcare professional before commencing any exercise regime. While every care has been taken in
the preparation of this material, the publishers and their respective employees or agents will not accept responsibility
for injury or damage occasioned to any person as a result of participation in the activities described in this book.

Contents

Workouts 144

Form & Function

The exercises in this book train the whole body. They are aimed at quality rather than quantity. Your goal is to do as many repetitions as you can while maintaining optimal form.

This type of training is for anyone inspired to get into shape from head to toe. It is for those who want to throw a ball harder, develop a smoother tennis stroke, or swim more laps—in the fast lane. It's also for people of any age or fitness level who want to feel good walking up stairs, running for the bus, or reaching for the top shelf—and cultivate a beautiful body along the way. The moves reflect real-life situations, incorporating lateral and horizontal movement to hone balance, flexibility, and stamina.

But why?

Why is form so important? Isn't calorie burn the same, regardless of how we move? Well, if you are sedentary, just getting off the couch and moving around—regardless of what you do or how you do it—will improve your fitness levels, and you should congratulate yourself for it. But when fitness is an integral and important part of your life, it makes sense to do it right. This is true for various reasons.

For one, good form is kinder to your spine. Form and function protect your body

from the back pain that can all too often accompany sudden bursts of exercise, not to mention the countless other movements like bending, lifting, and twisting that daily life demands.

Working a range of muscles at the same time helps to counteract muscular imbalance, a common condition in which one muscle becomes overdeveloped and compensates for other muscles, which then weaken—sometimes spurring discomfort and pain. For instance, if you attend spinning classes often and exclusively, you may find your quadriceps becoming stronger while your hamstrings only get a secondary challenge. This could lead to knee pain or problems. A remedy might be to add an exercise like the Dead Lift (page 80) to your routine to balance the new strength in your quads.

On top of all this, the total-body training technique of working multiple muscles as you focus on flexibility, balance, and range of motion gets you a better body. The multitasking approach helps you to tone up and get in shape more effectively, justifying those hours in the weight room or on the fitness mat.

Counteract muscular imbalance by adding complementary exercises to your routine.

Tips for Better Form

To give your form a boost, tune in to these tips. They apply to most exercises in this book.

• Avoid clenching or collapsing parts of your body. When performing Arm-Reach Plank (page 46), for instance, try adding a very subtle bend in your elbows so that your muscles, not your ligaments, do the work. And avoid locking your joints, whether they are joints you are moving or static ones. Your goal is dynamic engagement, rather than getting comfortable in a position and resting there.

• Pay attention to how you come out of each repetition. All too often, we lift weights above our heads and then let them fall down carelessly, jerking our spines and wasting a chance to strengthen arms and abs in the process. But coming out of an exercise is an opportunity to engage muscles, and paying attention to it maximises benefits and avoids injury.

• Aim for balance. For every abduction, your body will benefit from an adduction, and for every flexion, an extension. In this way you will develop muscles equally and to their full potential.

• If an exercise causes stress or strain, take a week or two off from performing it. Then, ease into it again at an easier level and see how your body reacts before increasing, for instance, the amount of added weight or the number of repetitions.

• In most exercises and in everyday life, picture your navel being pulled inward toward your spine. Your belly shouldn't bulge outward, but take care not to "suck in" either at the expense of proper breathing.

• Knee soreness is never desirable. Try placing a rolled-up blanket beneath your knees when kneeling or squatting, especially if contact with the floor feels uncomfortable. Never use a foam roller directly on your knees; instead, roll above or below the knee area.

• The muscles in your spine form a natural S-shaped curve. This is sometimes referred to as the neutral curve of your spine. Optimal posture involves supporting this neutral curve. When possible, therefore, your back should be neither hunched forward nor arched.

• Study how you sit, whether at the office or driving: do you lean to one side, stressing your abdomen or straining your lower back? You may need to add some lumbar support. If you find yourself twisting to one side, make a conscious effort to correct this imbalance through exercise. In addition to cultivating a sense of centeredness, this will help to prevent strain and possibly injury down the line.

• As a general rule, inhale to prepare, and then exhale as you carry out an action such as lifting or reaching. Soon you'll get a rhythm going, and will find that your breath helps you through your workout. Breathing while you move releases tension and affords you optimal control of your body. Deep inhalation and full exhalation exercises the lungs, increasing their capacity. Breathing, in short, benefits your functionality. Let your belly rise as you inhale and flatten as you exhale.

• Keep in mind that the myriad muscles in our bodies work together; when one fires, other parts of the body react. These exercises use numerous muscle groups along multiple planes of motion.

Study how you perform everyday tasks to see which functional training exercises can benefit you.

Fitness & Lifestyle

As a species, we evolved to move our bodies and to work hard to survive. The lack of physical effort needed to live today has led to a variety of physical and medical problems.

Through exercising regularly in a calm, controlled, and mindful way, we can learn to use our bodies more naturally. To see big benefits, aim for three 45-minute exercise sessions per week. Then, over time, try for even more: the results can be transformative, leading to lower cholesterol and body fat as well as a better mood.

Although the instructions in the following pages tell you to perform a certain number of repetitions, this is only a guideline and should not be the focus of your training. Instead, aim to carry out all of your repetitions with optimal form. If you feel your back arching, your abs bulging outward, or your arms flailing around, you may not be getting the most from the workout, regardless of how quickly you move or how many reps you complete.

Form and repetitions

If you're not racing through your Functional Burpees or banging out a bunch of Seated Russian Twists, then how do you measure progress in your fitness training?

Well, over time, you should experience an increase in the number of repetitions that you can carry out with proper form. For a person of average weight, performing 30 repetitions of an exercise like Mountain Climber exhausts muscles. Doing more and more reps with good form leads to muscle conditioning and greater endurance. Taking a short break between exercises brings your heart and your lungs into the work, helping you reap the cardiovascular benefits as well.

With form at the forefront of your mind, you can use the number of repetitions, and sometimes even speed, as a way to gauge your progress. Try asking yourself: is this becoming habit? Is my muscle memory getting ingrained with good habits, so that I feel a centeredness, flexibility, powerfulness, and even grace as I move through the daily tasks I used to ignore?

Try stretching a little more deeply each time you perform the Iliotibial Band Stretch.

Equipment

Various fitness tools can augment your fitness training. In the following pages, for instance, you'll encounter these pieces of equipment.

Medicine ball—a weighted ball used to strengthen and condition by adding weight to traditional exercises

Swiss ball—an inflatable ball used to engage pelvic and abdominal muscles as well as provide instability in exercise routines

Foam roller—a cylinder approximately 3 feet long by 6 inches wide used for releasing muscles

Body bar—a weighted bar, used for resistance training, stretching, and balancing

Step—a sturdy jump platform used for dynamic and plyometric exercise

Dumbbell and barbell—bars with weighted discs or balls at either end, used for muscle conditioning; a barbell is larger and heavier

Resistance band—a supple band that is often held taut and pulled against to enhance muscle-toning benefits of exercise

Resistance band

Barbell

Medicine ball

Swiss ball

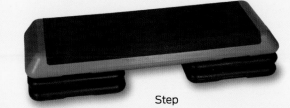

Body bar

Foam roller

Step

When you catch yourself engaging your core muscles, maintaining a neutral S-curve in your spine, or bending at the knees to pick up a box, you'll know your regimen is working. Aim for flexibility and a fuller range of motion; for example, at first, your palms may not be able to rest flat on the ground during an Iliotibial Band Stretch, but with practice you will reach further and further, until suddenly, there you are.

A fresh approach

Some of the exercises contain elements that may look familiar; however, it is worth taking time to revisit them. You may be tempted to rush through a set of Push-Up Walkouts, for instance—but tuning into the functionality of your muscles will help you rediscover the movement. It's worthwhile to watch yourself working out. Try looking into a mirror at first, or ask a friend about your form. Make sure your toes stay on the floor, your neck doesn't arch uncomfortably, and your belly stays pressed toward your navel with your abs engaged as you move. Think about the muscles in your arms, your legs, your core, and even your glutes staying engaged and working together—and you will likely feel the benefits of Push-Up Walkout in a new way.

Tuning in to form and muscle function makes exercises like Push-Up Walkout more fresh and effective.

Food as fuel

Diet is an important complement to your exercise regimen. As with your physical fitness efforts, think of diet in terms of what your food can do for your body. Beyond its myriad pleasurable qualities—very important!—food is there to fuel your lifestyle.

There is no one-size-fits-all way to eat healthily, as all bodies have individual needs. It is important to get regular blood tests to identify cholesterol levels

and determine whether you are getting enough of various vitamins. Also, try tuning in to your body's sensitivities: if you find yourself getting sleepy after lunch every day, the blood sugar spikes caused by the carbohydrates in your sandwich or the processed sugar in your dessert may be to blame. Experiment with dietary changes, bearing in mind that how you feel will have a direct effect on how much energy you can put into your exercise.

Healthy meal choices will complement your training regimen.

Weighty issues

This book is not about diet. However, for many of us, a top priority in starting to follow an exercise regimen is to get leaner. Bear in mind that a 1-pound weight loss involves a calorie deficit of 3,500. Shedding weight lies in burning more calories than we ingest. Alongside your exercise programm, try keeping a food journal. You may find that the simple act of recording your honest food intake exerts a big effect on how much you eat.

One tip: when a craving strikes, don't deprive yourself or "eat around" the craving. Instead, indulge—starting with a small portion of what you want. You know that feeling halfway through a big, indulgent meal when it stops being fun and you start to feel weighed down? Try pausing at that point. So often we lose track of our satiety levels; it actually takes our bodies 20 minutes to digest a meal and to fully register what we've eaten. You may find you can leave the rest of the meal.

Just as fitness training should be woven into everything you do, your diet should also work for your entire lifestyle and should not be so restrictive that you find it difficult to sustain it over the long term.

Treat Yourself Well

Listening to your body and responding to its needs is an important part of fitness training. Follow these tips to help your body function for you. Bonus: you'll combat exercise fatigue.

• Warm up. Run in place, dance, walk briskly down the street, set up an obstacle course in the kitchen—whatever gets your muscles warm will do the job. Aim for a minimum of 5 minutes, though 15 minutes is ideal.

• Keep breathing as you exercise. You'd be surprised how easy it is to hold your breath while working hard—in fact, it's natural to do so when performing a new or stressful task. And your breath can become shallow for numerous reasons; a sedentary lifestyle, anxiety, and nasal congestion can all play a role. If you catch yourself holding your breath or breathing shallowly, remind yourself to breathe fully, naturally and with a sense of ease.

• If injury occurs, use the exercises to help with healing. For instance, problems with the iliotibial (IT) band, the fibrous band that runs along the outside of your thigh from hip to knee, can cause lateral knee, hip, or back pain, so if you have pain there, make sure to include that stretch. In addition, many of these exercises and stretches can be incorporated into a physical therapy routine. Consult with your doctor or therapist to choose the proper exercises post-surgery or post-injury.

• Stay hydrated. If you start to feel thirsty, that means you are already approaching dehydration. Keep a water bottle within reach.

• After a workout, take time to cool down, stretch, and let your muscles release.

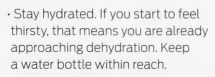

Hydration is an important part of any exercise routine. Keep a water bottle within reach.

Using this book

Consider this book your invitation to unlock the fitness of your whole body. Start with Body-Weight Exercises, paying attention to the performance tips given for each one. Once you feel comfortable with these, move on to the Added-Weight Exercises to tone your muscles, and finally to the Resistance Exercises to tone up. Practise the moves in the Stretching & Releasing chapter before, during, or after the other exercises. Choose moves for areas of your body that feel tight or painful under pressure; you may even feel some relief immediately after the exercise. Think of your body as a unified whole rather than a collection of unrelated parts. For instance, during Tensor Fasciae Latae Roll (pages 138–139), utilize the strength in your arms to modulate the amount of leg weight that is pushing into the roller.

Hip-to-Thigh Stretch

Each exercise has clear step-by-step instructions on how to perform it correctly. You will also find diagrams showing the main muscles that are called into play during the moves, but remember that this regimen works the body as a whole. As you work out, visualize your muscles not just "firing" to power the movement, but also staying engaged and dynamic. The sidebars contain information on the level of the exercise, the benefits it brings, and any physical problems to be aware of before doing the move.

At the end of the book is a series of suggested workouts, which will help you boost posture, transition from a long day at work to a night out, and more. Above all, this guide to fitness training is yours to explore. We wish you all the best.

Functional Burpee

Knee-Flexion
Ball Throw

Lying Abduction

Full-Body Anatomy

Annotation Key
* indicates deep muscles

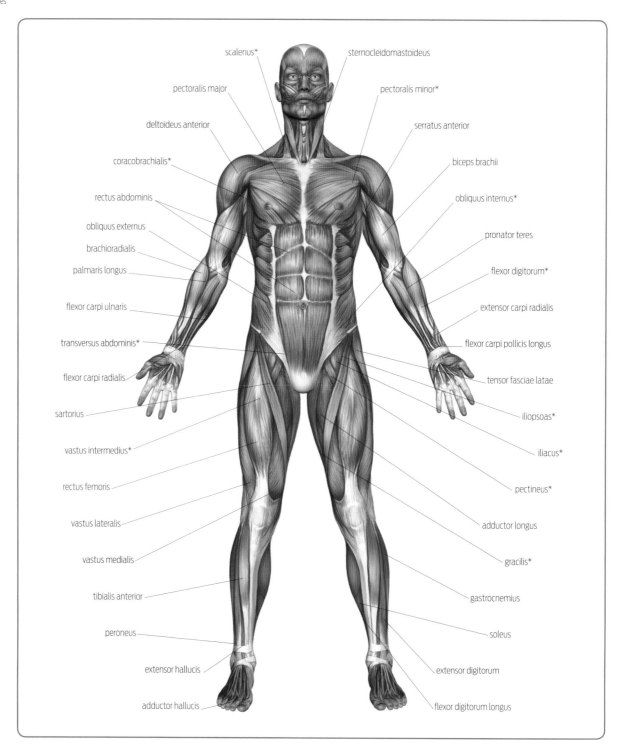

scalenus*

sternocleidomastoideus

pectoralis major

pectoralis minor*

deltoideus anterior

serratus anterior

coracobrachialis*

biceps brachii

rectus abdominis

obliquus internus*

obliquus externus

pronator teres

brachioradialis

flexor digitorum*

palmaris longus

extensor carpi radialis

flexor carpi ulnaris

flexor carpi pollicis longus

transversus abdominis*

tensor fasciae latae

flexor carpi radialis

iliopsoas*

sartorius

iliacus*

vastus intermedius*

pectineus*

rectus femoris

adductor longus

vastus lateralis

gracilis*

vastus medialis

gastrocnemius

tibialis anterior

soleus

peroneus

extensor digitorum

extensor hallucis

flexor digitorum longus

adductor hallucis

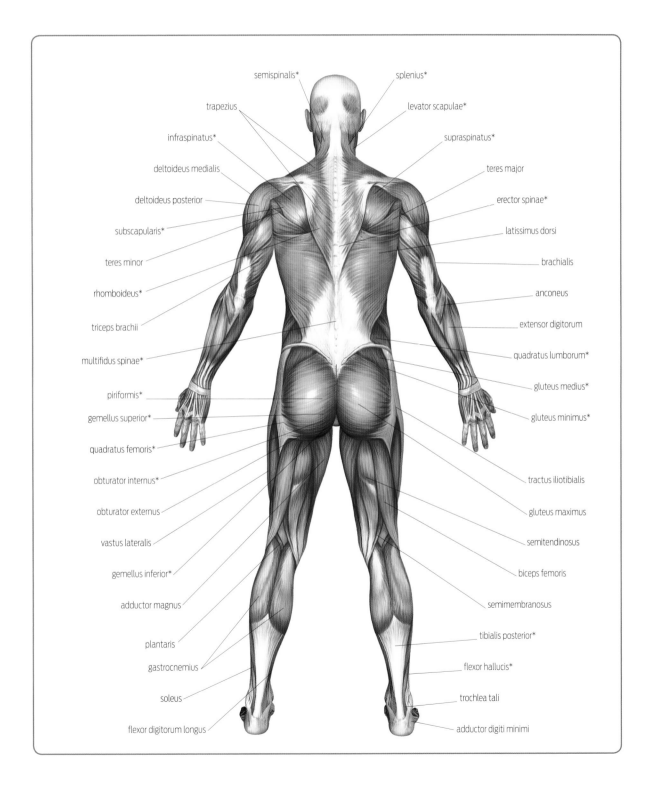

semispinalis*

splenius*

trapezius

levator scapulae*

infraspinatus*

supraspinatus*

deltoideus medialis

teres major

deltoideus posterior

erector spinae*

subscapularis*

latissimus dorsi

teres minor

brachialis

rhomboideus*

anconeus

triceps brachii

extensor digitorum

multifidus spinae*

quadratus lumborum*

piriformis*

gluteus medius*

gemellus superior*

gluteus minimus*

quadratus femoris*

obturator internus*

tractus iliotibialis

obturator externus

gluteus maximus

vastus lateralis

semitendinosus

gemellus inferior*

biceps femoris

adductor magnus

semimembranosus

plantaris

tibialis posterior*

gastrocnemius

flexor hallucis*

soleus

trochlea tali

flexor digitorum longus

adductor digiti minimi

Contents

Body-Weight Exercises

Moving your body effectively is key to total-body workout. Explore the following body-weight exercises before you move on to add weights or perform resistance moves. In time, they will build endurance, flexibility, strength, and stability—along with helping you to burn calories and tone muscles.

Remember to think of your body as a unified whole. Rather than isolating individual muscles as the rest of your body goes lax, you are aiming for total-body engagement with good form. Turn to the Workouts section (pages 144–157) to learn how to put them all together.

Warm-Up Obstacle Course

Whatever your plans, it is essential to warm up. This obstacle course provides an gentle warm-up for your body, while getting your mind engaged, too. You'll need to think about where you are placing your feet and keeping your balance, which improves coordination. Concentrate on doing each move correctly rather than rushing to complete the course.

1 Set up seven small objects on the floor, three to make a triangle and four a square.

2 Taking small, quick steps, step around all of the objects in the triangle.

Correct form
- Keep a steady pace as you move through the course.
- Take small steps, focusing on coordination.
- Stand upright.
- Keep your abdominal muscles pulled in and engaged.

Avoid
- Stopping at any point.
- Moving too quickly throughout the course.

3 Stand in front of the square and jump forward to land in the middle of the square. Complete a jumping jack.

4 Jump forward to land outside the square. Jog back to the beginning of the course and repeat.

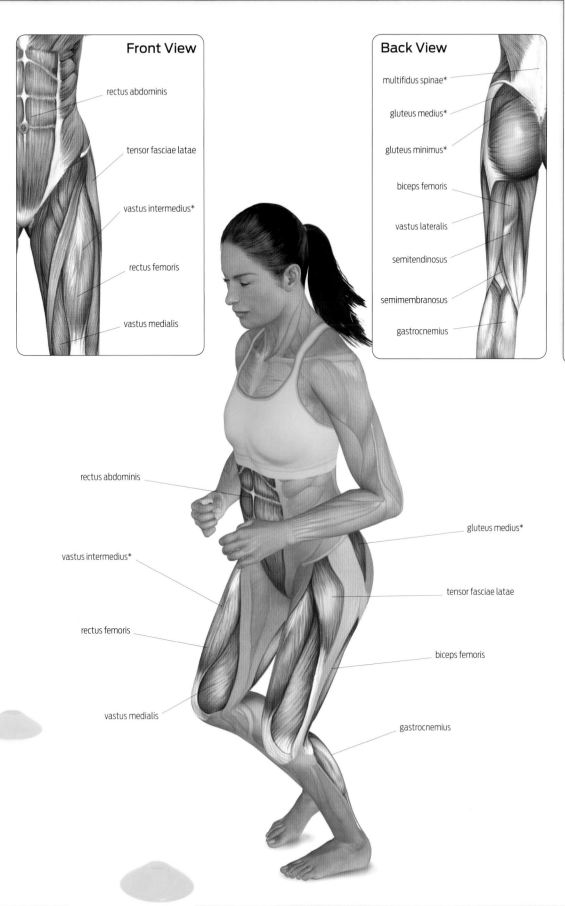

Front View

rectus abdominis

tensor fasciae latae

vastus intermedius*

rectus femoris

vastus medialis

Back View

multifidus spinae*

gluteus medius*

gluteus minimus*

biceps femoris

vastus lateralis

semitendinosus

semimembranosus

gastrocnemius

Level
· Beginner

Duration
· 3–5 minutes

Benefits
· Warms up all the muscles
· Improves agility

Caution
· Knee issues
· Ankle problems
· Lower leg pain

Annotation Key
* indicates deep muscles

rectus abdominis

gluteus medius*

vastus intermedius*

tensor fasciae latae

rectus femoris

biceps femoris

vastus medialis

gastrocnemius

Diagonal Reach

Perform this exercise to strengthen and stretch your abdominals, especially the oblique muscles. It also works your shoulder muscles. Aim for a smooth movement, creating a stretch across the body. Increasing the height of your reach will increase the stretch.

1 Stand with your feet hip-width apart and your arms at your sides.

2 Raise both arms upward and to the right to form a diagonal line. Follow your hands with your gaze. Return to starting position.

3 Repeat to the left side. Perform 12 repetitions.

Correct form
· Keep your abdominal muscles engaged.
· Keep your hips facing forward.
· Press your shoulders down.

Avoid
· Twisting your hips.
· Letting your abs bulge outward.
· Hunching your shoulders.
· Tensing your neck as you lift or lower your arms.

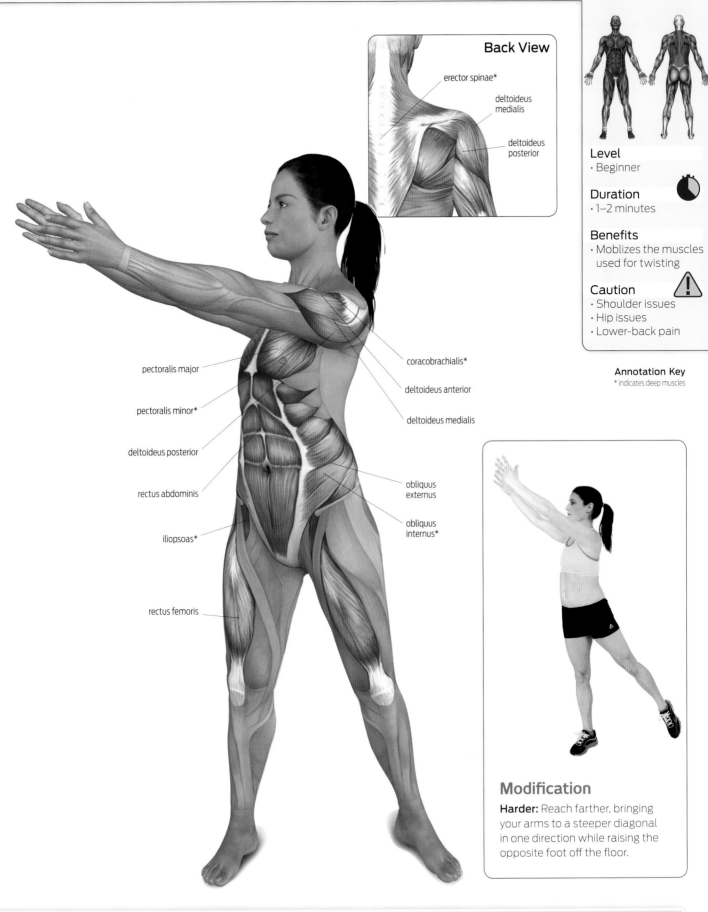

Back View

erector spinae*

deltoideus medialis

deltoideus posterior

Level
· Beginner

Duration
· 1–2 minutes

Benefits
· Moblizes the muscles used for twisting

Caution
· Shoulder issues
· Hip issues
· Lower-back pain

Annotation Key
* indicates deep muscles

pectoralis major

pectoralis minor*

deltoideus posterior

rectus abdominis

iliopsoas*

rectus femoris

coracobrachialis*

deltoideus anterior

deltoideus medialis

obliquus externus

obliquus internus*

Modification

Harder: Reach farther, bringing your arms to a steeper diagonal in one direction while raising the opposite foot off the floor.

Lateral-Extension Reverse Lunge

This Lunge works the lower body and legs, while increasing core stability. It is vital to make the step backward slowly and under control. Be aware of the muscles of your legs taking the weight of your body.

Correct form
· Keep your shoulders pressed downward.
· Keep your neck relaxed.
· Maintain upright form in your upper body as you lower and then raise your body.

Avoid
· Twisting either hip.
· Hunching your shoulders.
· Arching your back or hunching forward.

1 Stand with your feet hip-width apart and your arms at your sides or on your hips.

2 Step your right leg backward, flexing your foot so you are resting on your toes.

3 Bend both knees as you move into a lunge position. Lower your body, flexing your left knee and hip until your right leg is almost in contact with the floor. Raise your arms to the side until they are level with your shoulders.

4 Return to starting position by straightening the hip and knee of your left leg and bringing your right leg forward to meet your left.

5 Repeat on the opposite side. Alternating, complete 10 on each side.

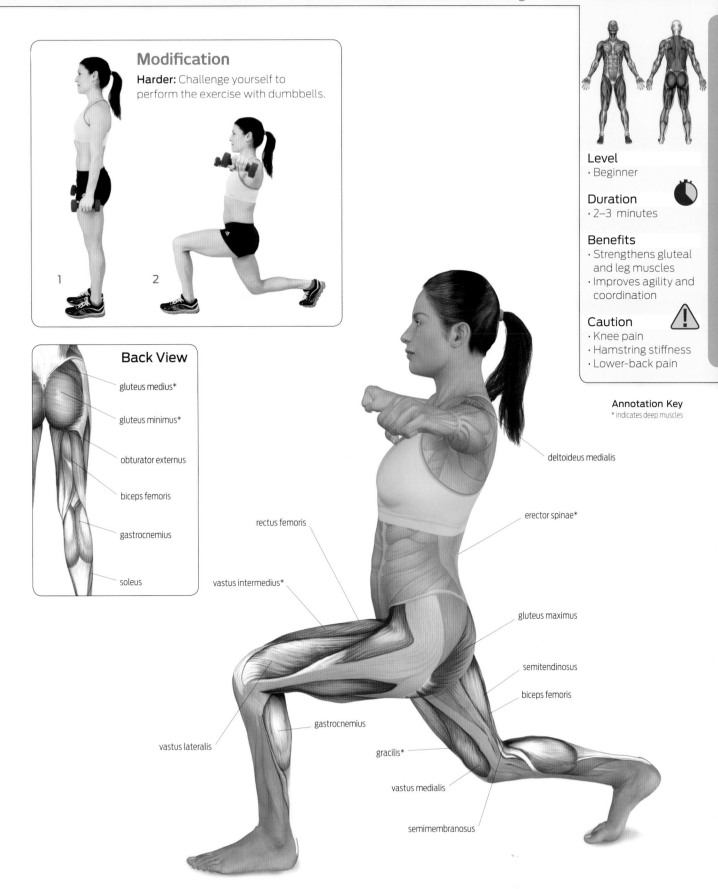

Modification

Harder: Challenge yourself to perform the exercise with dumbbells.

1

2

Back View

gluteus medius*

gluteus minimus*

obturator externus

biceps femoris

gastrocnemius

soleus

Level
· Beginner

Duration
· 2–3 minutes

Benefits
· Strengthens gluteal and leg muscles
· Improves agility and coordination

Caution
· Knee pain
· Hamstring stiffness
· Lower-back pain

Annotation Key
* indicates deep muscles

deltoideus medialis

rectus femoris

vastus intermedius*

erector spinae*

gluteus maximus

semitendinosus

biceps femoris

gastrocnemius

vastus lateralis

gracilis*

vastus medialis

semimembranosus

Chair Plié

This is a great exercise to perform at your desk to work your lower body and engage your inner thighs. Use it in conjunction with Chair Squat (pages 28–29) to improve your posture and tone the muscles of your lower body.

1 Stand with your feet in a wide stance, with toes turned out and the chair in front of you.

2 Keeping your knees aligned with your toes, bend your knees and lower your body into a squat position.

3 Keeping your back straight, raise yourself back to starting position. Perform 10 repetitions.

Correct form
· Keep your abdominal muscles pulled in.
· Keep your knees soft.
· Move gracefully and with control.

Avoid
· Turning your toes out to the point where it is uncomfortable.
· Twisting to either side.
· Arching your back or hunching forward.
· Losing your balance by moving in a jerky manner.

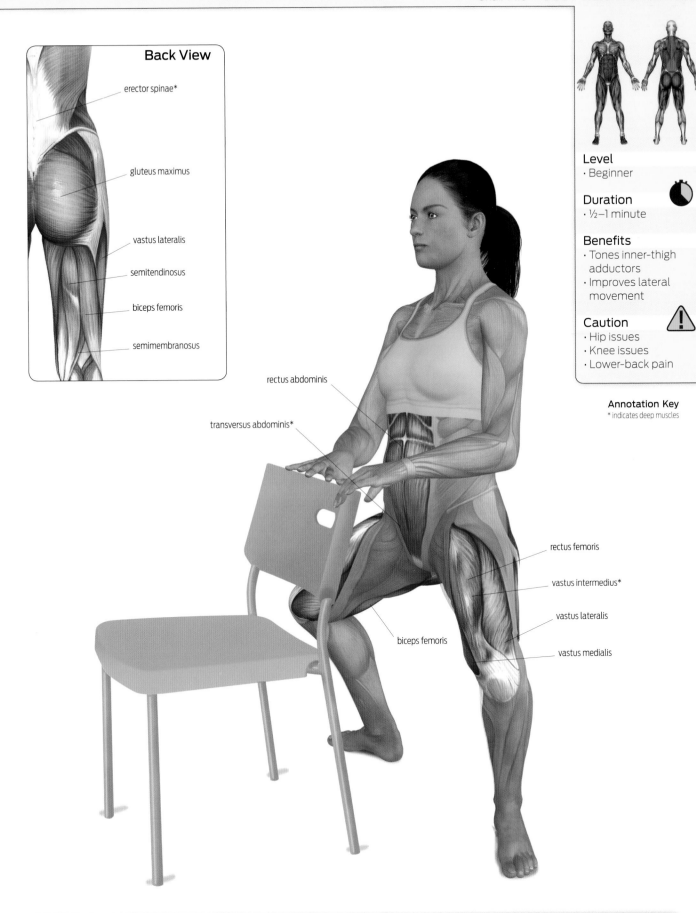

Back View

erector spinae*

gluteus maximus

vastus lateralis

semitendinosus

biceps femoris

semimembranosus

rectus abdominis

transversus abdominis*

rectus femoris

vastus intermedius*

vastus lateralis

vastus medialis

biceps femoris

Level
· Beginner

Duration
· ½–1 minute

Benefits
· Tones inner-thigh adductors
· Improves lateral movement

Caution
· Hip issues
· Knee issues
· Lower-back pain

Annotation Key
* indicates deep muscles

Chair Squat

Completing this exercise correctly means using your core properly. As well as engaging your leg muscles, it works nearly every muscle in your lower body and improves your posture.

1 Stand upright in front of the chair. Clasp your hands, and position them in front of your chest.

2 Slowly lower into a squat position.

3 Continue lowering until you are resting on the chair.

4 With control, rise back up to the starting position, and repeat, aiming for 10 repetitions.

Correct form
· Gaze forward.
· Keep your back straight.
· Engage your abs.

Avoid
· Arching your back or hunching forward.
· Tensing your neck.
· Hunching your shoulders.

Front View

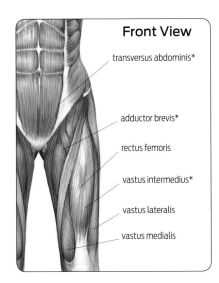

- transversus abdominis*
- adductor brevis*
- rectus femoris
- vastus intermedius*
- vastus lateralis
- vastus medialis

Modification

Harder: Challenge yourself by holding a Medicine Ball throughout the exercise.

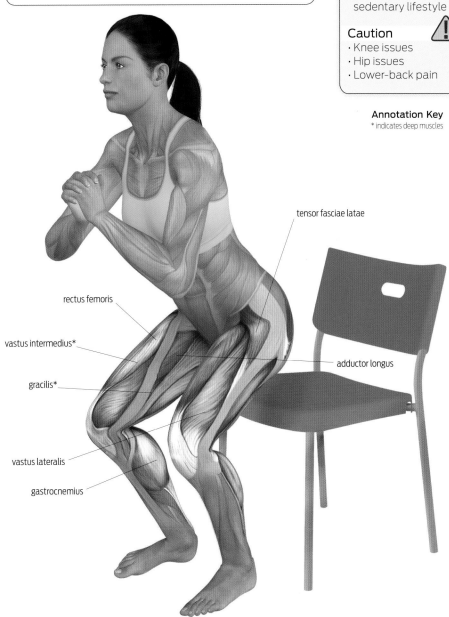

Level
- Beginner

Duration
- ½–1 minute

Benefits
- Restores mobility after injury
- Counteracts sedentary lifestyle

Caution
- Knee issues
- Hip issues
- Lower-back pain

Annotation Key
* indicates deep muscles

Back View

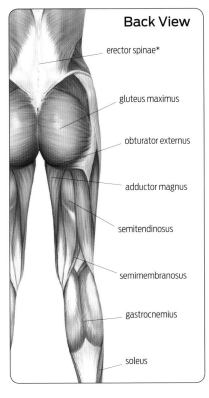

- erector spinae*
- gluteus maximus
- obturator externus
- adductor magnus
- semitendinosus
- semimembranosus
- gastrocnemius
- soleus

- tensor fasciae latae
- rectus femoris
- vastus intermedius*
- adductor longus
- gracilis*
- vastus lateralis
- gastrocnemius

Split Squat with Overhead Press

This is a good exercise for the lower body and legs. The Overhead Press can be made more effective by using weights, but avoid using this as a muscle-building exercise. Do the movement with power in your legs, feeling the muscles working together. Maintain a good posture.

1 Stand with your right leg behind you, with the ball of the foot resting on a step.

2 With your elbows bent to form right angles, raise both arms to shoulder height.

3 Bend both knees into a split squat position. Simultaneously, extend your arms over your head.

4 Return to starting position, and then repeat. Aim for 10 repetitions. Then, switch sides and perform 10 more repetitions with the other leg behind. If desired, repeat the whole sequence 2 more times.

Correct form
· Keep your back straight and your core upright.
· Press your shoulders back and down.

Avoid
· Arching your back as you raise your arms.
· Letting your abs bulge outward.
· Tensing your neck.

Modification

Harder: Hold dumbbells throughout the exercise.

Level
· Intermediate

Duration
· 1–2 minutes

Benefits
· Strengthens legs, including glutes, quads, and hamstrings
· Works trapezius
· Improves motion throughout body

Caution
· Leg problems
· Knee issues
· Lower-back pain

Annotation Key
indicates deep muscles

erector spinae*

gluteus medius*

gluteus minimus*

obturator externus

adductor magnus

biceps femoris

semitendinosus

semimembranosus

soleus

deltoideus posterior

deltoideus medialis

transversus abdominis*

pectineus*

adductor brevis*

rectus femoris

gluteus maximus

tensor fasciae latae

vastus medialis

gastrocnemius

gracilis*

vastus intermedius*

vastus lateralis

Functional Burpee

Burpees are aimed at improving strength and increasing aerobic fitness. Done slowly this movement builds power, but for aerobic intensity, it is best performed at a reasonably fast pace with a number of repetitions. Maintain form throughout each repetition; this becomes harder the more reps you do.

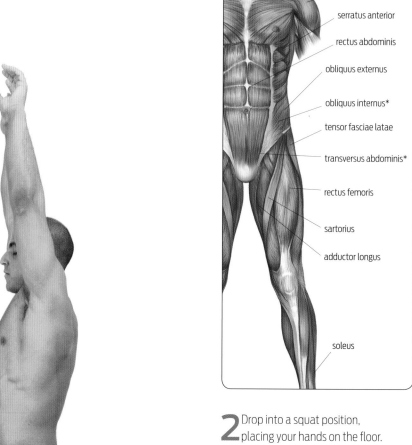

Front View

deltoideus anterior

serratus anterior

rectus abdominis

obliquus externus

obliquus internus*

tensor fasciae latae

transversus abdominis*

rectus femoris

sartorius

adductor longus

soleus

1 Stand with your feet hip-width apart and your arms above your head.

2 Drop into a squat position, placing your hands on the floor.

Correct form
- Make each movement cleanly with your body straight.
- Contract your abdominal muscles in the plank position.

Avoid
- Moving through the positions too quickly since this could reduce the effectiveness of the exercise.

3 In one quick motion, extend your feet back to assume a plank position.

4 In another quick motion, return to the squat position.

5 Stand up to starting position. Repeat, performing 15 repetitions.

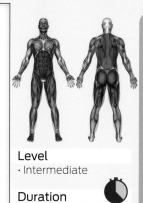

Level
· Intermediate

Duration
· ½–1 minute

Benefits
· Strengthens muscles
· Aids coordination

Caution ⚠
· Knee issues
· Lower-back pain

Annotation Key
* indicates deep muscles

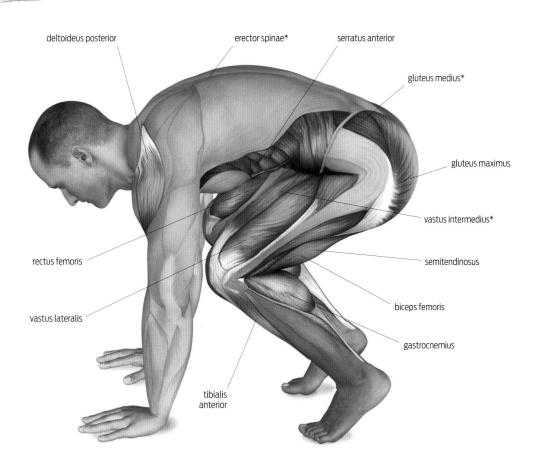

deltoideus posterior

erector spinae*

serratus anterior

gluteus medius*

gluteus maximus

vastus intermedius*

semitendinosus

biceps femoris

gastrocnemius

rectus femoris

vastus lateralis

tibialis anterior

Mountain Climber

This high-intensity exercise gets your heart rate going, improving your cardiovascular fitness, while it challenges your legs and core. It is an all-around exercise that also helps to develop muscular endurance in your upper arms and shoulders.

1 Begin in an upper push-up position, palms and toes on the floor.

2 Bring your right knee in toward your chest. Rest the ball of the foot on the floor.

3 Jump to switch feet in the air, bringing the left foot in and the right foot back. Continue alternating your feet as fast as you can safely go for 30 to 60 seconds.

Correct form
· As much as possible, keep your hands planted on the floor.
· Keep your shoulders pressed down.
· Maintain a quick pace.

Avoid
· Moving through the positions so quickly that you compromise your form.
· Hunching your shoulders.

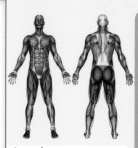

Back View

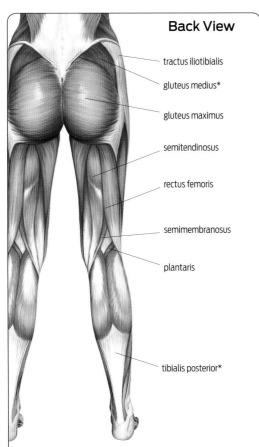

tractus iliotibialis

gluteus medius*

gluteus maximus

semitendinosus

rectus femoris

semimembranosus

plantaris

tibialis posterior*

Back View

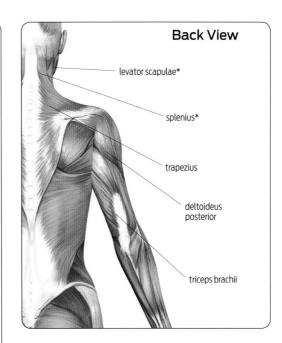

levator scapulae*

splenius*

trapezius

deltoideus posterior

triceps brachii

Level
· Beginner

Duration
· ½–1 minute

Benefits
· Improves muscle strength and body coordination

Caution
· Knee or hip issues
· Lower-back pain

Annotation Key
* indicates deep muscles

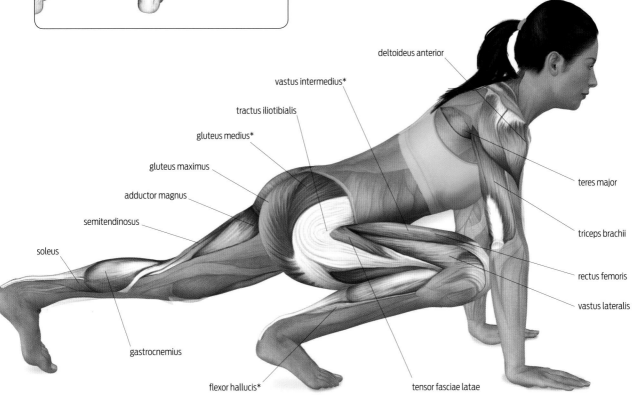

deltoideus anterior

vastus intermedius*

tractus iliotibialis

gluteus medius*

gluteus maximus

adductor magnus

semitendinosus

soleus

gastrocnemius

flexor hallucis*

tensor fasciae latae

teres major

triceps brachii

rectus femoris

vastus lateralis

Jumping Lunge

This is a cardiovascular exercise that combines a lower body workout with improving coordination and balance. It requires power in the quads and glutes, and the correct form is vital for toning the abs.

1 Stand upright, with your feet hip-width apart and your hands on your hips.

2 With your right leg, take a big step forward.

3 Bend both legs to lower into a deep lunge. Then, straighten both legs.

4 Jump up to switch legs so that your left leg is in front. Take a moment to find your balance.

5 Bend both knees to sink down into another lunge. Straighten your knees and then repeat, performing 10 repetitions.

Correct form
· Keep breathing throughout the exercise.
· Keep your front knee facing forward.
· Keep your torso upright.
· Maintain a steady pace.
· Gaze forward.

Avoid
· Allowing your front knee to twist to either side.
· Hunching your shoulders.
· Tilting your torso.
· Arching your back.

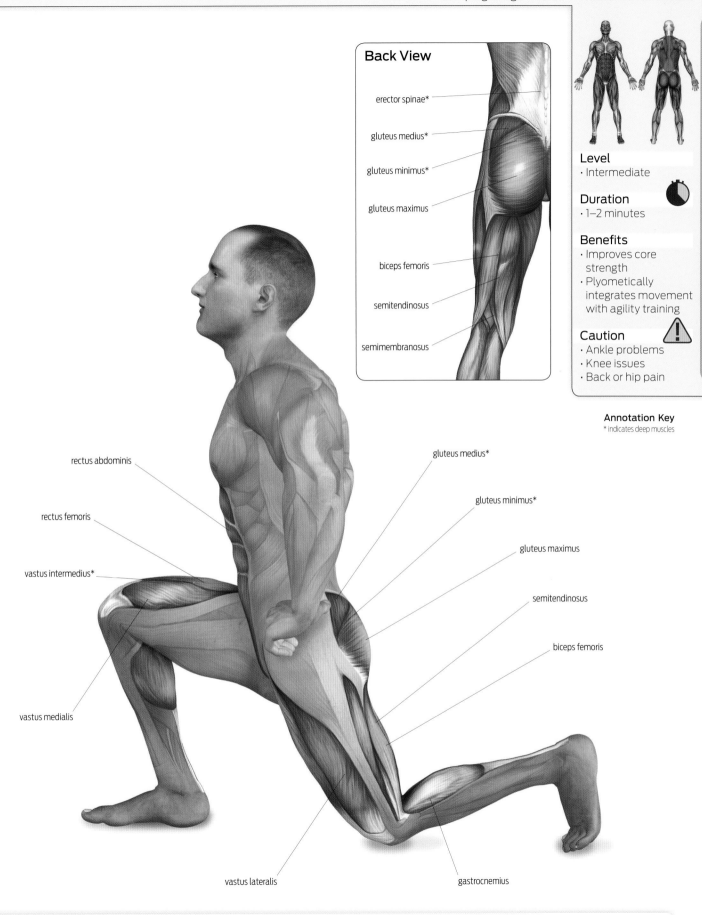

Back View

erector spinae*

gluteus medius*

gluteus minimus*

gluteus maximus

biceps femoris

semitendinosus

semimembranosus

Level
· Intermediate

Duration
· 1–2 minutes

Benefits
· Improves core strength
· Plyometically integrates movement with agility training

Caution
· Ankle problems
· Knee issues
· Back or hip pain

Annotation Key
* indicates deep muscles

rectus abdominis

gluteus medius*

rectus femoris

gluteus minimus*

vastus intermedius*

gluteus maximus

semitendinosus

biceps femoris

vastus medialis

vastus lateralis

gastrocnemius

Swiss Ball Jackknife

Swiss Ball Jackknife works the hip flexors and the shoulders and upper arms. It also targets both the front and back core muscles—especially your rectus abdominis and spinal erectors. Form is important since this is what gives the exercise its depth.

1 Kneel on your hands and knees, with the Swiss ball behind you. Your hands should be planted on the floor, with your arms straight.

2 One at a time, place your feet on the ball so that your legs are fully extended behind you and your body forms a line from head to toe. Find your balance.

3 Flex your hips, and pull your knees toward your chest, driving your hips toward the ceiling and retracting your abdomen.

Correct form
- Engage your core, keeping your abs pulled inward.
- Keep your back as straight as possible.
- Keep your body stable throughout.
- When your legs are extended on the ball, keep legs, torso, and neck in a straight line.
- Relax your neck.

Avoid
- Arching your back or neck.
- Letting your stomach bulge outward.

4 Continuing to engage your abs, pull the ball further toward you. Maintain form in your upper body as you raise your buttocks toward the ceiling.

5 Hold for 5 seconds. Then, straighten your legs to the starting position. Begin with 10 repetitions, working up to 20.

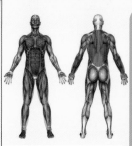

Level
· Intermediate

Duration
· 1–3 minutes

Benefits
· Improves agility and coordination
· Strengthens core

Caution
· Lower-back issues
· Shoulder pain

Annotation Key
* indicates deep muscles

obliquus externus

transversus abdominis*

obliquus internus*

iliopsoas*

erector spinae*

tensor fasciae latae

rhomboideus*

latissimus dorsi

rectus abdominis

teres major

rectus femoris

deltoideus posterior

tibialis anterior

biceps brachii

pectoralis major

triceps brachii

flexor carpi ulnaris

Leg-Extension Chair Dip

The Chair Dip is a powerful upper body exercise that concentrates on increasing the strength of your core, shoulders, and arms. Make sure to do slow, controlled movements to ensure the intensity of each step.

1 Sit on the very edge of a chair, with your palms on the seat. Your back should be straight, your knees bent to form 90-degree angles.

2 Slowly and with control, engage your abdominal muscles and press your palms into the seat as you move your buttocks forward and lower slightly so that you are no longer resting on the chair

3 Bending your arms slightly, extend your left leg forward to form a straight line.

4 Return your foot to the floor. Repeat on the other side, working up to 10 repetitions per side. Release and return to starting position.

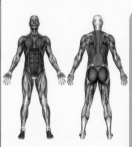

Back View

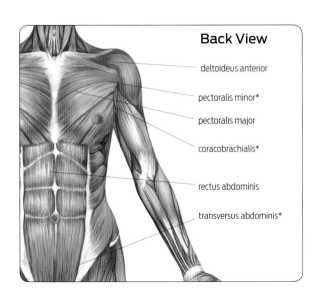

- deltoideus anterior
- pectoralis minor*
- pectoralis major
- coracobrachialis*
- rectus abdominis
- transversus abdominis*

Correct form
· Keep your supporting foot anchored to the floor.
· Keep your back straight.
· Keep your hips level.
· Gaze forward.

Avoid
· Arching your back or hunching forward.
· Twisting your hips.

Level
· Beginner

Duration
· 1–2 minutes

Benefits
· Improves balance
· Strengthens core and triceps

Caution
· Back issues
· Shoulder pain

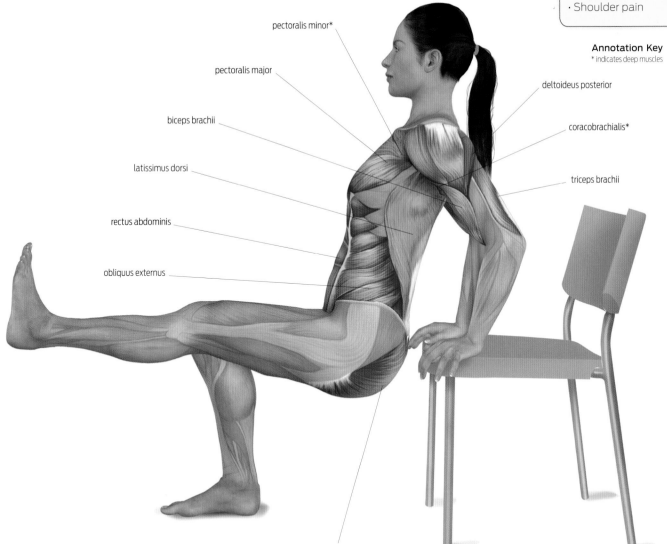

Annotation Key
* indicates deep muscles

- pectoralis minor*
- pectoralis major
- biceps brachii
- latissimus dorsi
- rectus abdominis
- obliquus externus
- deltoideus posterior
- coracobrachialis*
- triceps brachii
- gluteus maximus

One-Legged Step-Down

A strong core and good posture are required for this exercise, which targets all the muscles used for balance. Slow, correct movements will give your muscles the best workout. Remember to keep your abs tight and your shoulders back.

1 Stand on a step, facing forward.

Correct form
· Use the wall or a rail for support if desired.
· Move slowly and with control.
· Focus on maintaining good form.

Avoid
· Allowing your knee to twist inward; instead, keep it in line with your middle toe.
· Rushing through the movement.

2 Bend your right leg. Simultaneously step your left leg downward, flexing the foot to rest on your heel.

3 Without rotating your torso or knee, press upward through your right leg to return to starting position. Switch legs and repeat, performing 20 repetitions.

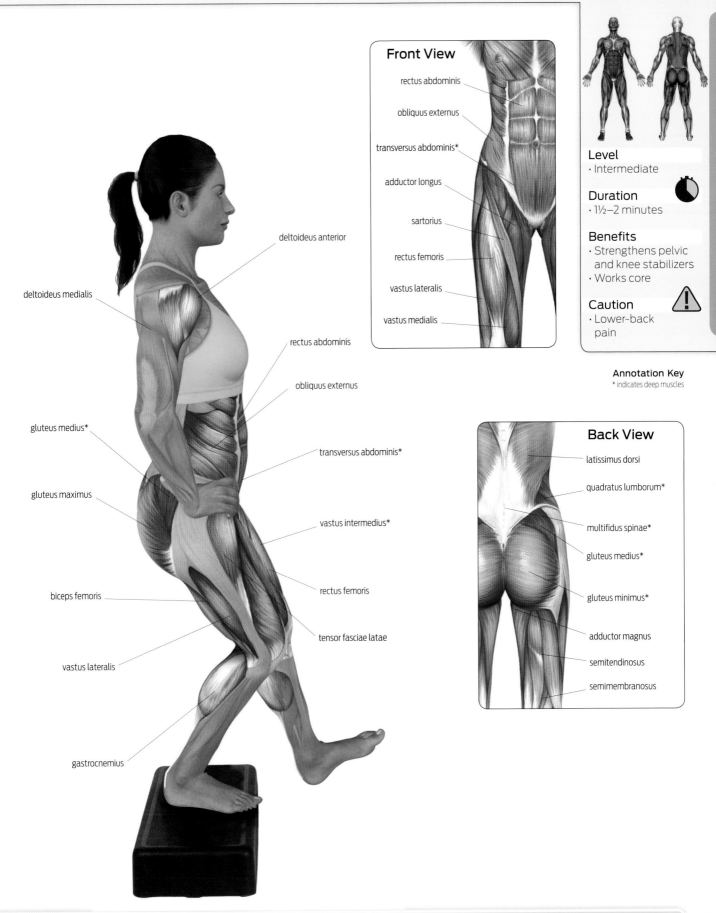

Front View

rectus abdominis

obliquus externus

transversus abdominis*

adductor longus

sartorius

rectus femoris

vastus lateralis

vastus medialis

Level
· Intermediate

Duration
· 1½–2 minutes

Benefits
· Strengthens pelvic and knee stabilizers
· Works core

Caution
· Lower-back pain

Annotation Key
* indicates deep muscles

deltoideus anterior

deltoideus medialis

rectus abdominis

obliquus externus

gluteus medius*

transversus abdominis*

gluteus maximus

vastus intermedius*

biceps femoris

rectus femoris

tensor fasciae latae

vastus lateralis

gastrocnemius

Back View

latissimus dorsi

quadratus lumborum*

multifidus spinae*

gluteus medius*

gluteus minimus*

adductor magnus

semitendinosus

semimembranosus

Push-Up Walkout

Balance and controlled power are in this exercise, which focuses on strenthening all the key muscle groups of the torso, shoulder, arms, and upper legs. Good form is vital.

1 Stand with your feet hip-width apart.

2 Bend forward until your hands reach the floor.

3 "Walk" your hands out in front of you as far as possible.

4 Press your palms into the floor and tuck your toes so that you are in an upper push-up position. Perform a push-up.

5 "Walk" your hands back toward your feet. Work up to 10 repetitions.

6 Roll back up to starting position.

Correct form
· Keep your feet planted on the floor as you "walk" your hands forward and back.
· Keep your back in a neutral position while performing the push-up.
· Pull your stomach in and engage your abdominal muscles.

Avoid
· Arching your back or hunching forward.
· Going too far forward at first; instead, build up to the full walkout if desired.
· Tensing your neck.

Front View

pectoralis major

pectoralis minor*

coracobrachialis*

biceps brachii

quadratus lumborum*

gluteus minimus*

gluteus maximus

tensor fasciae latae

tractus iliotibialis

erector spinae*

biceps femoris

latissimus dorsi

trapezius

rectus abdominis

serratus anterior

pectoralis major

brachialis

triceps brachii

Level
• Intermediate

Duration
• 1–3 minutes

Benefits
• Strengthens and tones core, chest, and back muscles

Caution
• Lower-back pain
• Wrist pain
• Shoulder problems

Annotation Key
* indicates deep muscles

Modification

Easier: To make the push-up less strenuous at first, bend your legs and rest your knees on the floor.

Arm-Reach Plank

Variations on the Plank rely on stillness, rather than movement. Keep your body and legs as still as you can while lifting your arm. Try to maintain your balance evenly over your body, rather than transferring it to the arm on the floor.

1 Begin face-down, resting on your forearms and knees.

2 One at a time, step your feet back into a plank position. Engage your abdominal muscles and find a neutral spine.

3 Maintaining proper plank form, slowly lift your right arm off the floor. Hold for 30 seconds. Release and return to starting position.

4 Switch arms and repeat. Aim to hold for 60 seconds as you become stronger.

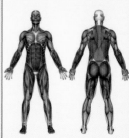

Modification

Easier: Instead of raising each arm fully off the floor, lift only your forearm. Additionally, try bending your knees to make the exercise less strenuous.

1

2

Level
· Intermediate

Duration
· 2–6 minutes

Benefits
· Improves balance
· Strengthens and tones arms, legs, and abdominal muscles

Caution
· Neck issues
· Arm or shoulder injury

Annotation Key
* indicates deep muscles

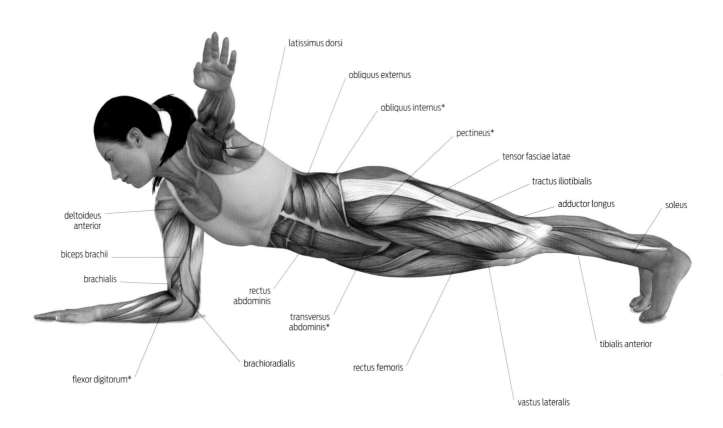

latissimus dorsi

obliquus externus

obliquus internus*

pectineus*

tensor fasciae latae

tractus iliotibialis

adductor longus

soleus

deltoideus anterior

biceps brachii

brachialis

rectus abdominis

transversus abdominis*

tibialis anterior

brachioradialis

rectus femoris

flexor digitorum*

vastus lateralis

Twisting Knee Raise

Calling for balance and coordination, along with flexibility and core strength, the Twisting Knee Raise provides a good cardiovascular workout. It also tones the quads and calves and builds on the power of the abs.

1 Stand with your feet hip-width apart and your arms at your sides. Raise both arms and bend your elbows so that each arm forms a right angle, palms facing forward.

2 Raise your left knee toward your abdomen. At the same time, bring your right elbow toward the knee. Aim for your knee and elbow to touch.

Correct form
· Keep your abs engaged and contracted.
· Maintain a quick pace.
· Face forward as you perform the twist.

Avoid
· Hyperextending your back.
· Letting your hips twist excessively.

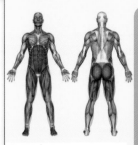

Front View

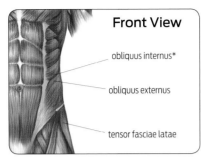

obliquus internus*

obliquus externus

tensor fasciae latae

Level
· Intermediate

Duration
· 2–3 minutes

Benefits
· Improves balance
  and coordination
· Strengthens and
  tones core muscles,
  quads, and calves

Caution
· Hip or leg
  issues

Annotation Key
* indicates deep muscles

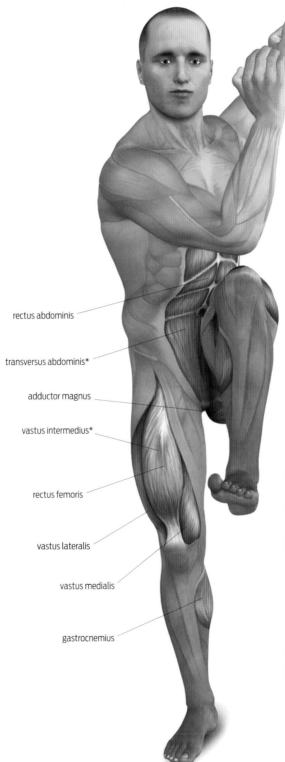

rectus abdominis

transversus abdominis*

adductor magnus

vastus intermedius*

rectus femoris

vastus lateralis

vastus medialis

gastrocnemius

3 Return to starting position.
Repeat, alternating sides.
Aim for 20 repetitions.

Back View

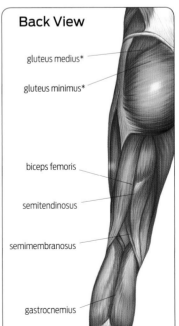

gluteus medius*

gluteus minimus*

biceps femoris

semitendinosus

semimembranosus

gastrocnemius

Heel Beat

This exercise focuses on toning the glutes but also works the abs and legs. Good form is important to gain maximum benefit. Keep the upper body relatively relaxed; it is easy to tense it in an attempt to maintain balance.

1 Lie facedown with your forearms on the floor. Rest your hips on top of a small Swiss ball. Extend your legs behind you.

2 Turn your legs out from the top of your hips.

3 Pull your navel up toward your spine, pressing your pubic bone into the ball. Lengthen your legs and lift them off the mat.

4 Press your heels together and then separate them in a rapid but controlled motion.

5 Beat your heels together for 8 counts. Release and then repeat, performing 6 repetitions.

Correct form
· Press your shoulders down toward your back.
· Squeeze your thigh muscles while lifting your legs.
· Squeeze your buttocks and abs.
· Keep your breathing steady.

Avoid
· Hunching your shoulders.
· Tensing your neck.

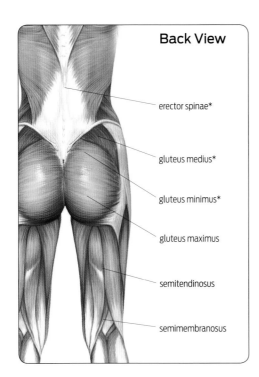

Back View

- erector spinae*
- gluteus medius*
- gluteus minimus*
- gluteus maximus
- semitendinosus
- semimembranosus

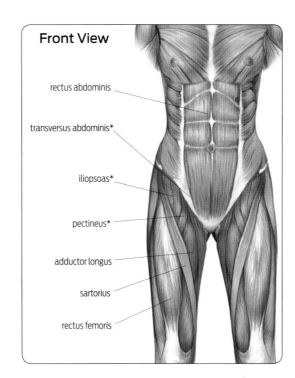

Front View

- rectus abdominis
- transversus abdominis*
- iliopsoas*
- pectineus*
- adductor longus
- sartorius
- rectus femoris

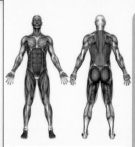

Level
- Beginner

Duration
- 2–3 minutes

Benefits
- Tones abs and glutes
- Stablises core
- Lengthens extension muscles
- Aids coordination

Caution
- Back issues
- Shoulder injury

Annotation Key
* indicates deep muscles

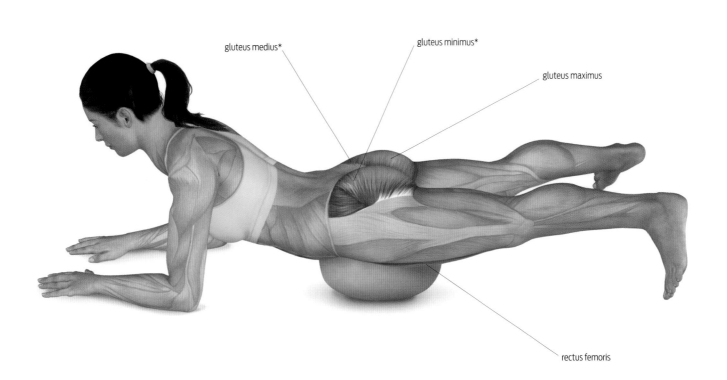

- gluteus medius*
- gluteus minimus*
- gluteus maximus
- rectus femoris

Swimming

An exercise that is a challenge for your coordination, Swimming is a strengthening workout that targets the shoulders, the whole of the back, and the back of the thighs. Make sure you feel the sides of your torso working as you lift your arms.

1 Lie on your stomach with your legs hip-width apart. Stretch your arms beside your ears on the floor. Engage your pelvic floor, and draw your navel into your spine.

2 Lift your left arm and right leg simultaneously. Raise your head slightly off the floor.

3 Lower your arm and leg to the starting position, maintaining a stretch in your limbs.

4 Repeat on the other side. Aim for 8 repetitions.

Correct form
· Relax your neck.
· Keep your glutes tightly squeezed.
· Draw your navel toward your spine.
· Press your shoulders down and back.
· Extend your limbs as long as possible in opposite directions.
· Keep your resting arm and leg on the floor.

Avoid
· Tensing your neck.
· Lifting your shoulders toward your ears.

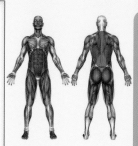

Modification

Harder: Lift your arms and legs at the same time, and move them as if you were making snow angels. Keep your abs engaged and your back neutral as you move.

1

2

Level
· Beginner

Duration
· 1–2 minutes

Benefits
· Stabilizes core
· Tones abs
· Strengthens hip and
  spinal extensors
· Stabilizes spine

Caution
· Back pain
· Shoulder issues

Annotation Key
* indicates deep muscles

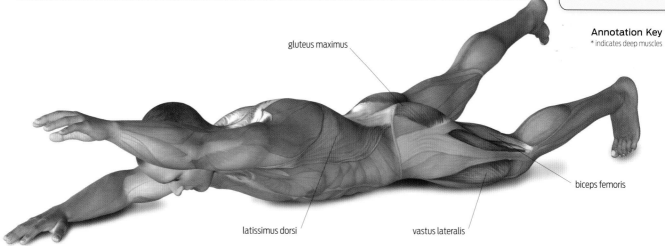

gluteus maximus

biceps femoris

latissimus dorsi

vastus lateralis

Back View

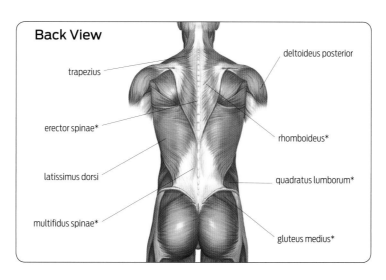

trapezius

deltoideus posterior

erector spinae*

rhomboideus*

latissimus dorsi

quadratus lumborum*

multifidus spinae*

gluteus medius*

Piriformis Bridge

This powerful stretching exercise works on the key muscle groups around the core, including the glutes and abs. It also creates a gentle stretch on the iliotibial band and will improve flexibility in this area over time.

1 Lie on your back, arms extended at your sides. Your knees should be bent, with feet on the floor.

2 Keeping the rest of your body still, raise your right leg to rest the ankle on your left knee

Correct form
· Squeeze your buttocks as you lift and lower.
· Draw your navel toward your spine.
· Press your shoulders down toward your back.
· Anchor your arms to the floor.
· Relax your neck.

Avoid
· Tensing your neck.
· Lifting your shoulders toward your ears.

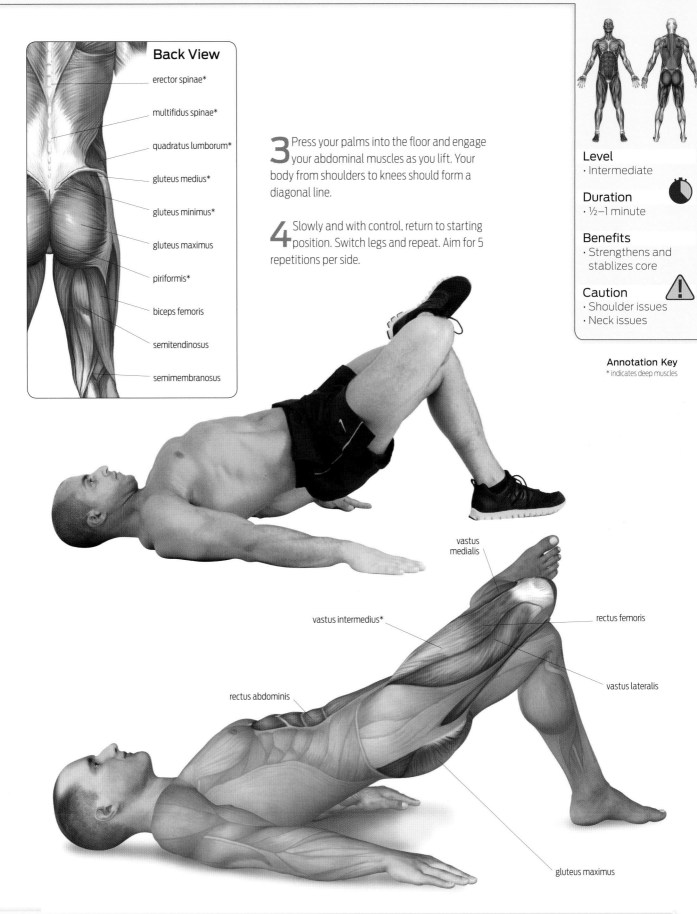

Back View

erector spinae*

multifidus spinae*

quadratus lumborum*

gluteus medius*

gluteus minimus*

gluteus maximus

piriformis*

biceps femoris

semitendinosus

semimembranosus

3 Press your palms into the floor and engage your abdominal muscles as you lift. Your body from shoulders to knees should form a diagonal line.

4 Slowly and with control, return to starting position. Switch legs and repeat. Aim for 5 repetitions per side.

Level
· Intermediate

Duration
· ½–1 minute

Benefits
· Strengthens and stablizes core

Caution
· Shoulder issues
· Neck issues

Annotation Key
* indicates deep muscles

vastus medialis

vastus intermedius*

rectus femoris

vastus lateralis

rectus abdominis

gluteus maximus

Swiss Ball Bridging Raise

This is a high intensity exercise for the core, pelvis, glutes, upper legs, and hamstrings. Only hold the position under control. If you start to wobble, release, return your body to the mat, and repeat. With practice, you will be able to hold the raise for longer.

Correct form
· Keep your back in a neutral position.
· Press your shoulders down your back.
· Engage your abdominal muscles.

Avoid
· Hunching your back.
· Tensing your shoulders or neck.
· Letting the Swiss ball wobble.

1 Lie face-up on the floor with your arms at your sides and your lower legs resting on the Swiss ball.

2 Press your palms into the floor and engage your abdominal muscles as you lift your upper body off the floor. Your body should form a diagonal line. If desired, hold for a few seconds.

3 Slowly and with control, lower back to starting position. Repeat, performing 10 repetitions.

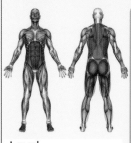

Back View

erector spinae*

multifidus spinae*

quadratus lumborum*

gluteus medius*

gluteus minimus*

piriformis*

semitendinosus

semimembranosus

Level
· Intermediate

Duration

· ½–1 minute

Benefits
· Stabilizes and works pelvis and core
· Strengthens glutes and hamstrings

Caution
· Shoulder issues
· Neck issues

Annotation Key
* indicates deep muscles

Modification

Harder: In the raised position, lift one leg off the ball, extending it upward while maintaining your form. Return to starting position. Repeat on the other side, keeping both legs straight and your back neutral as you move.

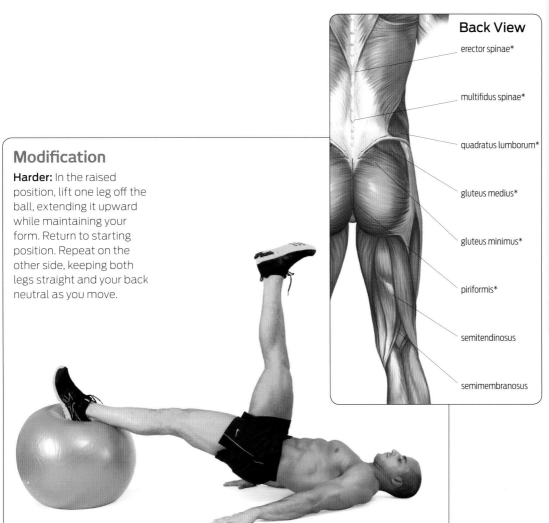

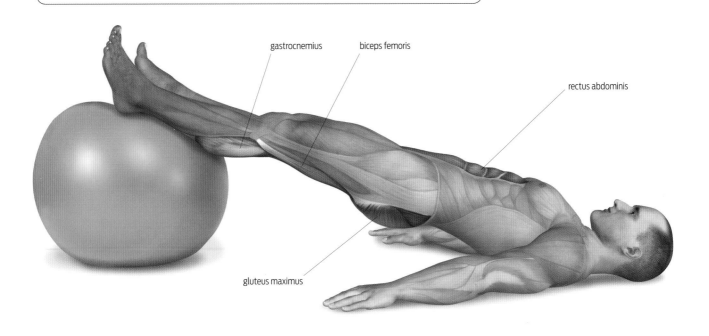

gastrocnemius

biceps femoris

rectus abdominis

gluteus maximus

Chin-Up with Hanging Leg Raise

This intense exercise is aimed at increasing upper body strength while working on producing a strong set of abdominal muscles. It also works the quads. The more you engage your core, the more powerful the workout.

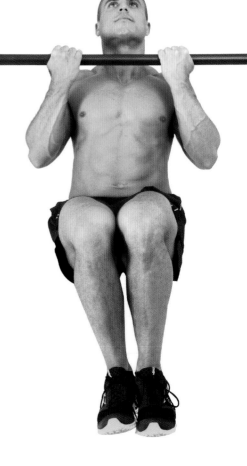

Correct form
- Keep your feet together as you raise your knees.
- Keep your movement slow and controlled.
- Engage your core muscles throughout this challenging exercise.

Avoid
- Moving in a jerky manner.
- Arching your back.
- Tensing your neck.

1 Begin hanging from a chin-up bar, gripping it firmly with both hands.

2 Use your arm muscles to lift yourself up, aiming to bring your chin over the bar.

3 With your abdominal muscles strongly engaged, raise your knees. Hold for as long as possible.

4 Slowly straighten your legs. Then, straighten your arms as you return to starting position.

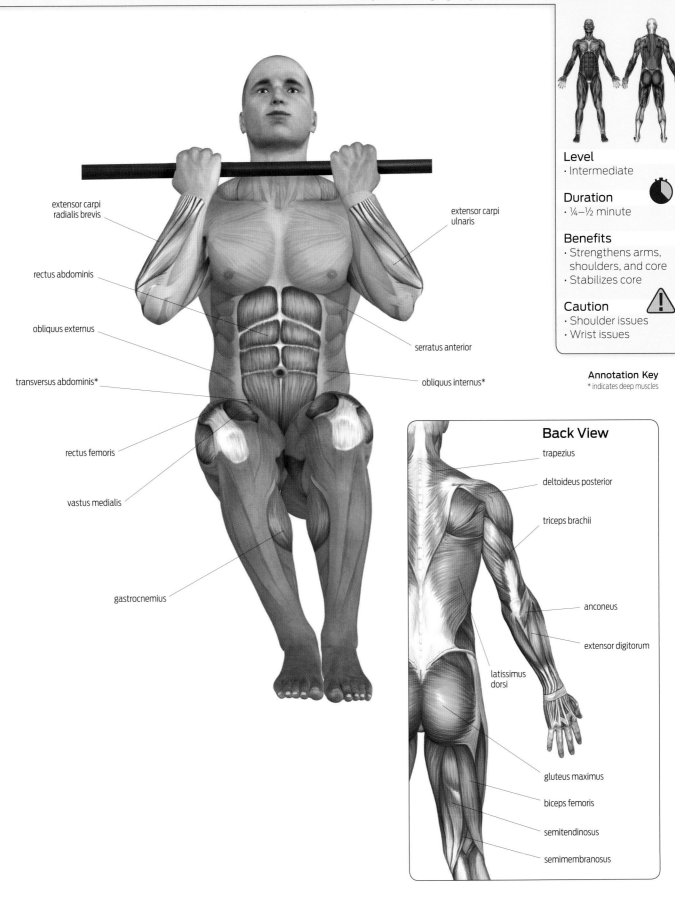

Level
· Intermediate

Duration
· ¼–½ minute

Benefits
· Strengthens arms, shoulders, and core
· Stabilizes core

Caution
· Shoulder issues
· Wrist issues

Annotation Key
* indicates deep muscles

extensor carpi radialis brevis

extensor carpi ulnaris

rectus abdominis

obliquus externus

serratus anterior

transversus abdominis*

obliquus internus*

rectus femoris

vastus medialis

gastrocnemius

Back View

trapezius

deltoideus posterior

triceps brachii

anconeus

extensor digitorum

latissimus dorsi

gluteus maximus

biceps femoris

semitendinosus

semimembranosus

Full-Body Roll

The key to this exercise is to work slowly and gently increase the stretch without risking strain on the lower-back area. The stretch occurs mainly in the obliques but you will also feel it through the glutes.

Correct form
· Keep your abdominal muscles, especially your obliques, engaged as you roll.
· Keep your legs straight.
· Move at a steady pace.

Avoid
· Rushing through the movement.

1 Lie on your back, with your arms extended at your sides and your legs extended on the floor.

2 Turn your head to the right and raise your right leg straight upward so that it is perpendicular to the floor.

3 Slowly rotate your lower body to the left, lowering your right leg until your foot is just above the floor.

4 Roll your lower body and leg back then lower your leg to the starting position.

5 Repeat, alternating sides for 8 repetitions.

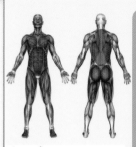

Back View

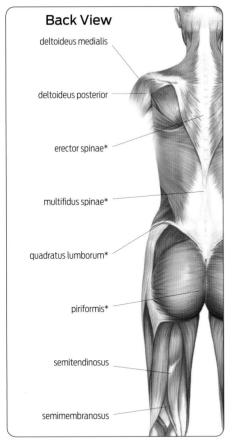

- deltoideus medialis
- deltoideus posterior
- erector spinae*
- multifidus spinae*
- quadratus lumborum*
- piriformis*
- semitendinosus
- semimembranosus

Front View

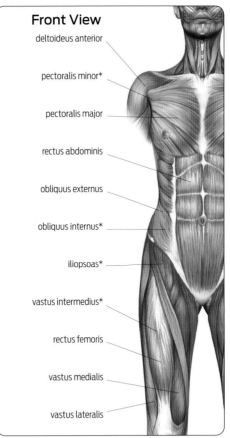

- deltoideus anterior
- pectoralis minor*
- pectoralis major
- rectus abdominis
- obliquus externus
- obliquus internus*
- iliopsoas*
- vastus intermedius*
- rectus femoris
- vastus medialis
- vastus lateralis

Level
- Intermediate

Duration

- 1–2 minutes

Benefits
- Tones core muscles, especially obliques
- Stretches glutes and latissimus dorsi

Caution ⚠
- Lower-back pain
- Hip issues

Annotation Key
* indicates deep muscles

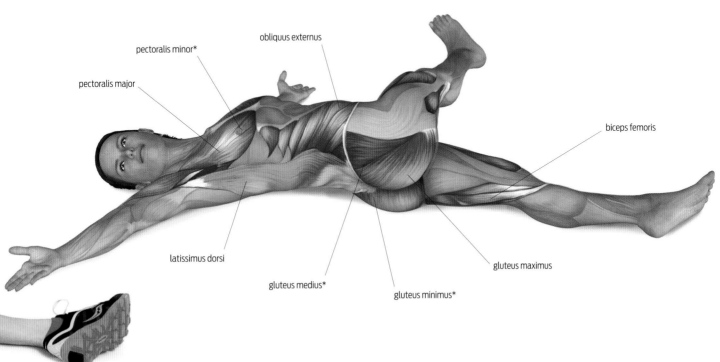

- pectoralis minor*
- pectoralis major
- obliquus externus
- biceps femoris
- latissimus dorsi
- gluteus medius*
- gluteus minimus*
- gluteus maximus

Contents

Added-Weight Exercises

In the weight room, functional training takes an unusual route to fitness, eschewing the "exercise to fatigue" adage in favor of, well, mixing it up. If you notice your previously pristine form suffering—your back arching while you hold Dead Lift, for example—don't power through. Instead, pause, change position, and do a different exercise, then return to the Dead Lift. You'll find you approach it with better form. Zoom through a set of repetitions and you'll miss out on the good stuff: the spinal integrity, core stability, and muscle engagement and dynamism that will help you excel at life's challenges.

Reach-and-Twist Walking Lunge

Adding the Medicine ball to the Lunge, and incorporating a twist into the movement, makes this exercise a challenge for coordination and balance, along with improving core and lower body strength.

1 Stand with feet roughly hip-width apart and your torso facing forward. Hold a weighted Medicine ball in both hands.

2 Lunge your left foot forward. Begin to bend both knees, lowering your whole body into the lunge. At the same time, raise the Medicine ball until it is over your left shoulder, held in both hands.

Correct form
- As much as possible, keep your torso facing forward.
- Keep your abdominal muscles engaged.
- Move smoothly.

Avoid
- Hunching your shoulders.
- Arching your back.
- Turning your neck in either direction.
- Letting your belly bulge outward.
- Losing control of the Medicine ball.
- Holding the Medicine ball more with one hand than the other.

3 In a single motion, rise up to stand, bring the ball back to center, and then perform the lunge and reach in the other direction.

4 Continue to lunge and move the ball from side to side as you walk forward. Do this for 15 steps.

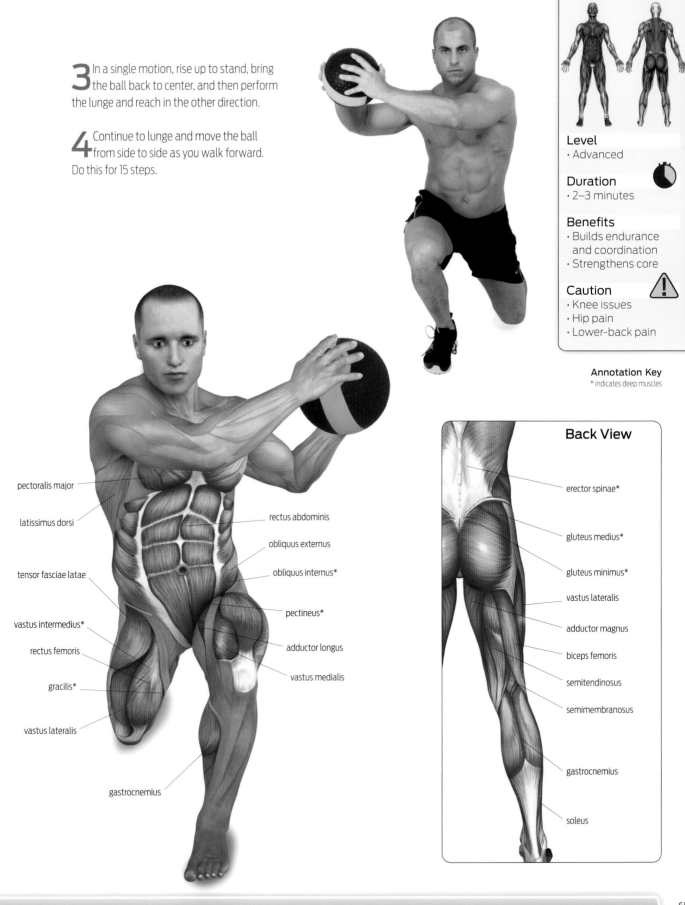

Level
· Advanced

Duration
· 2–3 minutes

Benefits
· Builds endurance and coordination
· Strengthens core

Caution
· Knee issues
· Hip pain
· Lower-back pain

Annotation Key
* indicates deep muscles

pectoralis major

latissimus dorsi

rectus abdominis

obliquus externus

obliquus internus*

tensor fasciae latae

pectineus*

vastus intermedius*

adductor longus

rectus femoris

vastus medialis

gracilis*

vastus lateralis

gastrocnemius

Back View

erector spinae*

gluteus medius*

gluteus minimus*

vastus lateralis

adductor magnus

biceps femoris

semitendinosus

semimembranosus

gastrocnemius

soleus

Clean-and-Press

This is a good basic weight exercise to tone and strengthen the upper body. Excellent posture throughout is important to ensure both sides of your upper body are worked equally and that you do not risk an injury. Enjoy the feeling of moving with fluidity and grace.

1 Begin in a high squatting position so that your upper legs are parallel with the floor. Hold the body bar in front of you, arms straight.

2 Using the muscles in your legs as well as your abdominals, rise to stand as you bend your arms to bring the bar to shoulder height. If you choose, extend one foot in front of the other.

3 Move your feet to parallel position, hip-width or wider apart, and bring the body bar above your head. Hold for several seconds.

4 Focus on breath and alignment as you bring the bar down to shoulder height in a controlled manner.

5 Repeat the lift overhead and the controlled lowering, aiming for 10 repetitions.

Correct form
· Your back should be in a neutral S-curve position during all steps of the exercise.
· Engage your legs and core muscles as you rise to stand.
· While you raise the bar overhead, keep your abdominals strongly engaged.

Avoid
· Hunching your shoulders.
· Letting your abdominals bulge outward.
· Distorting the S-curve of your spine by arching your back or hunching forward.
· Rushing through the movement.

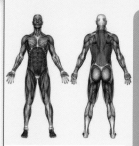

Level
· Beginner

Duration
· 2–3 minutes

Benefits
· Strengthens and
  tones the whole
  body

Caution
· Shoulder issues
· Wrist issues
· Lower-back pain

Annotation Key
* indicates deep muscles

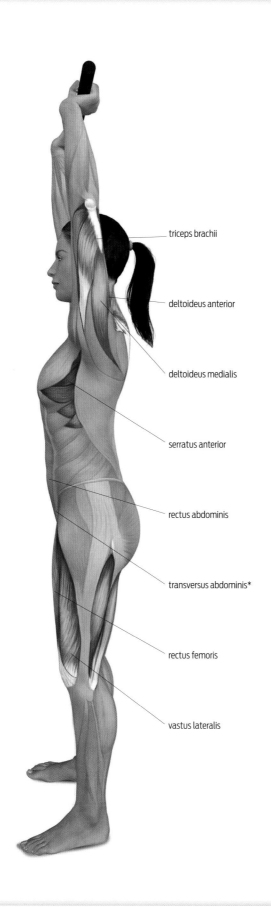

triceps brachii

deltoideus anterior

deltoideus medialis

serratus anterior

rectus abdominis

transversus abdominis*

rectus femoris

vastus lateralis

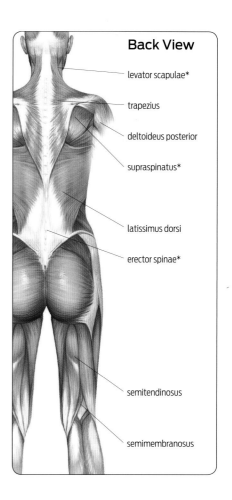

Back View

levator scapulae*

trapezius

deltoideus posterior

supraspinatus*

latissimus dorsi

erector spinae*

semitendinosus

semimembranosus

Knee-Flexion Ball Throw

Introducing full body movement into weight-based exercises helps to improve balance and coordination while toning a wide range of muscles. This exercise can provide an aerobic workout when done for several minutes.

1 Hold a weighted Medicine ball in front of your chest, taking a few steps forward to get ready if you choose.

2 Prepare to throw the ball by positioning your left foot behind you, heel off the floor. Keeping your torso stable, raise the ball until it is positioned above your right shoulder.

Correct form
· Gaze forward.
· Keep your torso facing forward.
· Engage your abdominal muscles as you throw.

Avoid
· Excessively twisting your torso to either side.
· Hunching your shoulders.

3 Bend the knee of your back foot to lift it off the ground as you throw the ball forward.

4 Retrieve the ball (or have someone toss it back to you). Then, repeat on the opposite side, performing 10 throws.

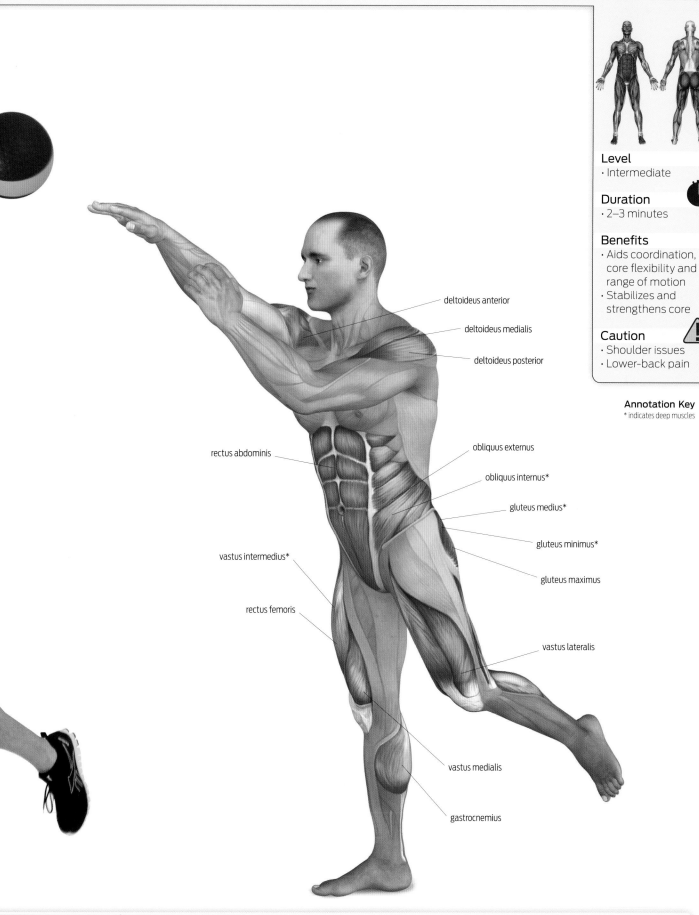

Level
· Intermediate

Duration
· 2–3 minutes

Benefits
· Aids coordination, core flexibility and range of motion
· Stabilizes and strengthens core

Caution
· Shoulder issues
· Lower-back pain

Annotation Key
* indicates deep muscles

deltoideus anterior

deltoideus medialis

deltoideus posterior

rectus abdominis

obliquus externus

obliquus internus*

gluteus medius*

gluteus minimus*

gluteus maximus

vastus intermedius*

rectus femoris

vastus lateralis

vastus medialis

gastrocnemius

Heel Raise with Overhead Press

Focusing on the shoulders and abs, this simple exercise also includes a basic stretch and workout for the calves and ankle joints.

1 Stand with your feet hip-width apart and your arms at your sides, a dumbbell in each hand.

2 Raise your arms, bending your elbows and lifting until the dumbbells are at ear height.

Correct form
· Keep your torso facing forward.
· Pull your abdominal muscles inward.
· Raise and lower your arms smoothly and with control.
· Gaze forward.
· Keep your back in a neutral position, envisioning your spine lengthening as you lift your heels.
· Use your core muscles to help you balance while heels are lifted.

Avoid
· Tilting or twisting your torso.
· Hunching your shoulders.
· Arching your back or hunching forward.
· Holding your breath while in the lifted position.

Modification
Easier: Bring your arms to ear level only as you raise your heels. Try holding for a few seconds before you release.

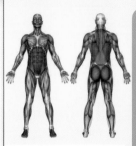

3 Bring your weights overhead as you lift your heels off the floor to stand on your tiptoes. Balance for a few seconds, if desired.

4 Lower your heels to the floor and bring your arms back to starting position. Repeat, aiming for 15 repetitions with good form.

Level
· Intermediate

Duration
· 2–3 minutes

Benefits
· Strengthens and tones shoulders, triceps, and calves

Caution
· Ankle issues
· Wrist and shoulder pain
· Lower-back pain

Annotation Key
* indicates deep muscles

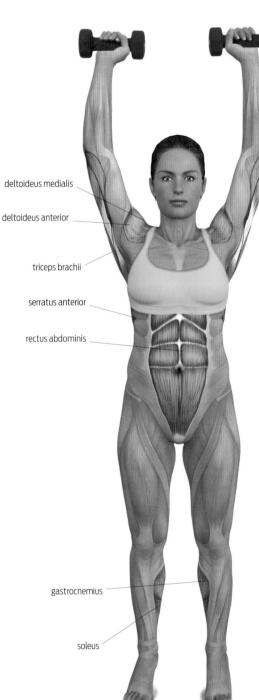

deltoideus medialis

deltoideus anterior

triceps brachii

serratus anterior

rectus abdominis

gastrocnemius

soleus

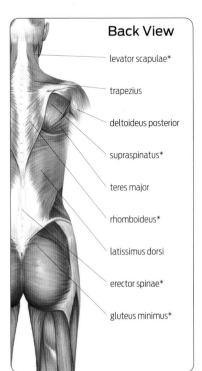

Back View

levator scapulae*

trapezius

deltoideus posterior

supraspinatus*

teres major

rhomboideus*

latissimus dorsi

erector spinae*

gluteus minimus*

Lateral-Extension Lateral Lunge

A complementary exercise to the Lateral-Extension Reverse Lunge (pages 24–25), the Lateral Lunge introduces a powerful workout for the upper leg muscles and strengthens the shoulders, too. Keep the movements controlled and fairly slow.

1 Stand with your feet hip-width apart and your arms at your sides, a dumbbell in each hand.

2 Take a big step to the left, and then bend your left knee to assume a side lunge position. At the same time, raise both arms so that they are parallel to the floor, forming a straight line.

3 Smoothly and with control, return to the starting position.

4 Repeat on the other side, working up to 10 repetitions on alternating sides.

Correct form
· Keep your torso facing forward as you lunge to the side.
· Pull your abdominal muscles inward.
· Gaze forward.

Avoid
· Positioning one arm in front of the other in the raised position.
· Hunching your shoulders.
· Arching your back or hunching forward.
· Twisting your torso to either side.

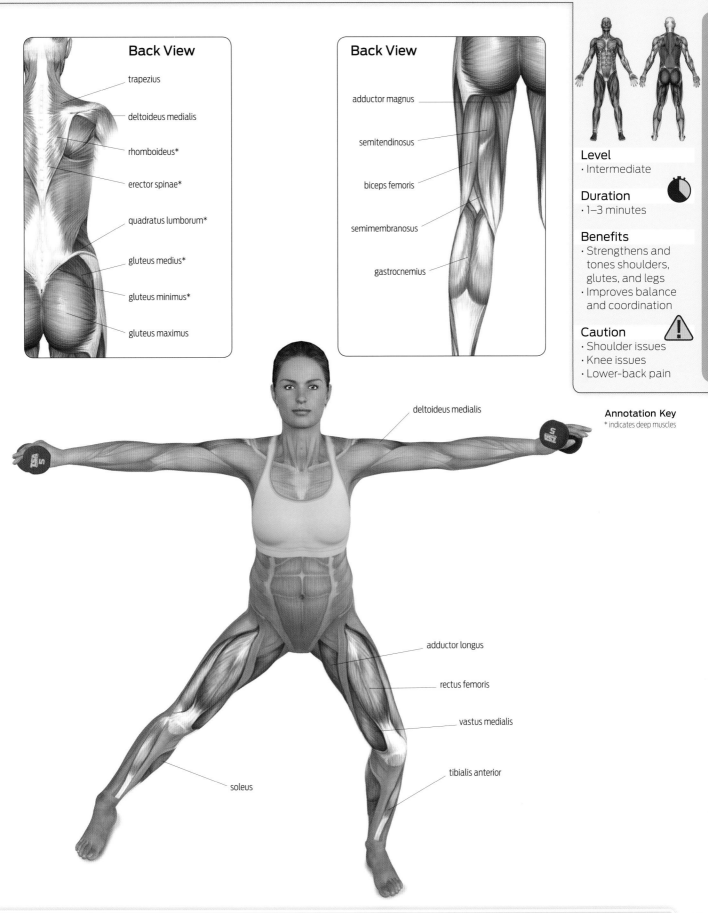

Back View

- trapezius
- deltoideus medialis
- rhomboideus*
- erector spinae*
- quadratus lumborum*
- gluteus medius*
- gluteus minimus*
- gluteus maximus

Back View

- adductor magnus
- semitendinosus
- biceps femoris
- semimembranosus
- gastrocnemius

Level
· Intermediate

Duration
· 1–3 minutes

Benefits
· Strengthens and tones shoulders, glutes, and legs
· Improves balance and coordination

Caution
· Shoulder issues
· Knee issues
· Lower-back pain

Annotation Key
* indicates deep muscles

deltoideus medialis

adductor longus

rectus femoris

vastus medialis

tibialis anterior

soleus

Curling Step-and-Raise Lunge

During this exercise, the actions of moving laterally on and off the step while lifting the dumbbells give your coordination and balance a workout, while the knee and dumbbell raises are a test for your core tone and strength.

Correct form
· Keep your upper arms stationary as you curl and release.
· Keep your movements smooth and controlled.
· Keep your torso facing forward.
· Pull your abdominal muscles inward.
· Gaze forward.
· Press your shoulders away from your ears.

Avoid
· Twisting your neck.
· Hunching your shoulders.
· Arching your back or hunching forward.
· Rushing through the movement.

1 Stand with your feet hip-width apart and your arms at your sides, a dumbbell in each hand. Position a step beside your left foot.

2 Place your left foot on the step.

3 Shift your weight onto your left foot. Bend your elbows, curling the dumbbells toward your chest. At the same time, raise your right knee as the foot comes off the floor. Continue raising and curling until your right leg forms a right angle and your dumbbells are nearly at shoulder height.

4 Lowering the dumbbells, cross your right leg in front of your left leg, lowering it to the floor, left of the platform. Simultaneously bend your left leg.

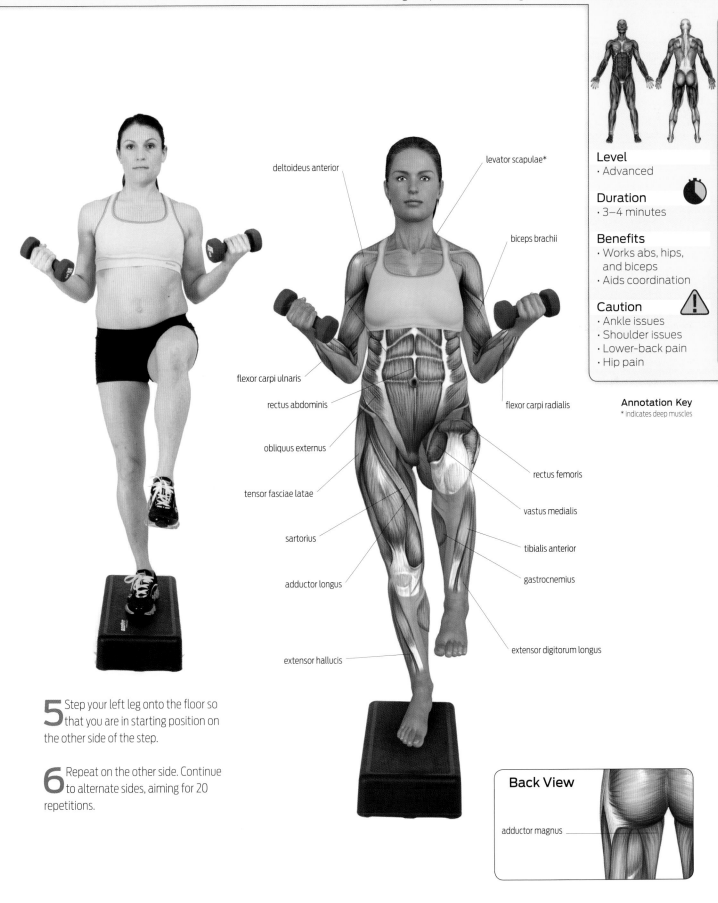

deltoideus anterior

levator scapulae*

biceps brachii

flexor carpi ulnaris

rectus abdominis

flexor carpi radialis

obliquus externus

tensor fasciae latae

rectus femoris

vastus medialis

sartorius

tibialis anterior

adductor longus

gastrocnemius

extensor hallucis

extensor digitorum longus

Level
· Advanced

Duration
· 3–4 minutes

Benefits
· Works abs, hips, and biceps
· Aids coordination

Caution
· Ankle issues
· Shoulder issues
· Lower-back pain
· Hip pain

Annotation Key
* indicates deep muscles

5 Step your left leg onto the floor so that you are in starting position on the other side of the step.

6 Repeat on the other side. Continue to alternate sides, aiming for 20 repetitions.

Back View

adductor magnus

Figure 8

The key to this exercise is fluid and well-balanced movement. Perform it slowly and deliberately, allowing your arms to feel the full weight of the ball in each position, rather than rushing through it.

1 Stand with your feet hip-width apart or slightly wider. Grasp a Medicine ball in both hands, and hold it in front of your torso.

2 Shift your weight to the right. In a smooth, controlled movement, extend both arms and bring the Medicine ball toward the lower right side of your body.

3 Continue shifting your weight to the right, bringing the left heel off the floor if desired as you raise the ball toward the upper right side of your body.

Correct form
· Follow the ball's movement with your gaze.
· Keep your core muscles engaged and your abs pulled inward.
· Anchor both feet to the floor.

Avoid
· Straining your neck.
· Tensing or hunching your shoulders.
· Arching your back or hunching forward.
· Rushing through the movement.

Figure 8 • ADDED-WEIGHT EXERCISES

deltoideus anterior

deltoideus medialis

deltoideus posterior

rectus abdominis

obliquus externus

obliquus internus*

biceps femoris

Back View

semitendinosus

biceps femoris

semimembranosus

Level
· Intermediate

Duration
· 2–3 minutes

Benefits
· Improves flexibility, and range of motion
· Stabilizes core

Caution
· Shoulder issues
· Lower-back pain

Annotation Key
* indicates deep muscles

4 In a Figure 8 motion, bring the ball diagonally toward the lower left side of your body, and then raise it to the upper left as you shift your weight onto your left leg

5 Repeat 5 times in this direction. Then, switch directions and repeat.

Knee Raise with Lateral Extension

Balance and tone are required for this power-building exercise. Aim to keep your shoulders level when lifting your leg—it is all too easy to allow the shoulder to tilt.

1 Stand with your feet hip-width apart and your arms at your sides, a dumbbell in each hand.

2 Shifting weight onto your left leg, bend your right knee and raise the leg. At the same time, raise your arms until the weights are slightly below shoulder height. Take a moment or two to find your balance.

Correct form
· Keep your torso facing forward as much as possible.
· Pull your navel toward your spine and engage your abdominal muscles.
· Gaze forward.
· Maintain a neutral S-curve in your spine.
· Anchor your standing leg to the floor.
· Keep breathing.

Avoid
· Twisting your torso to either side.
· Letting your abs bulge outward.
· Arching your back or hunching forward.

3 Keeping your arms and upper body stationary, extend your right leg out to the side. Try holding for a few seconds.

4 Moving with control, lower your arms and return your right leg to starting position.

5 Repeat on the other side. Alternating sides, begin with 5 repetitions on each side before working up to 10.

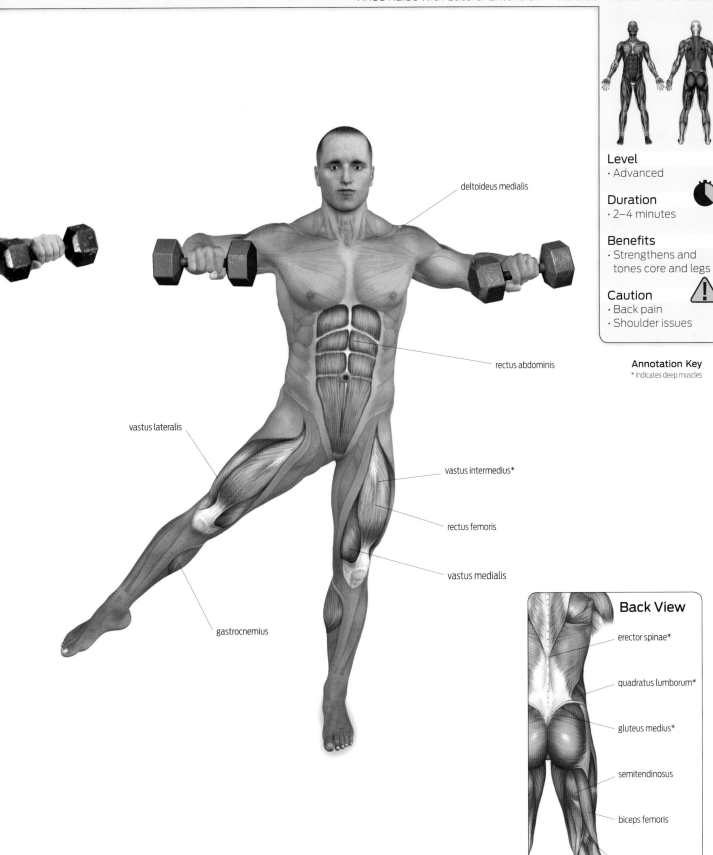

deltoideus medialis

rectus abdominis

vastus lateralis

vastus intermedius*

rectus femoris

vastus medialis

gastrocnemius

Level
· Advanced

Duration
· 2–4 minutes

Benefits
· Strengthens and tones core and legs

Caution
· Back pain
· Shoulder issues

Annotation Key
* indicates deep muscles

Back View

erector spinae*

quadratus lumborum*

gluteus medius*

semitendinosus

biceps femoris

semimembranosus

Dead Lift

A classic added-weight exercise, the Dead Lift can be made easier by using lighter weights and more difficult with heavier weights. As with all the exercises, it is vital to maintain a good posture and to use the correct muscles for lifting. If necessary, reduce the weight and increase the reps.

1 Stand with your feet shoulder-width apart, with a barbell at your feet. Lean over to grasp the weight with both hands.

2 Using your core muscles as well as your arms, raise the barbell, hingeing at the hips as you slowly rise to a standing position.

3 Smoothly return the barbell to the floor, again hingeing at the hips. Repeat, starting with 3 repetitions before building up to 10.

Correct form

- Maintain a slight bend in your knees if desired.
- As much as possible, maintain a neutral S-shaped spinal position as you lift and lower.
- Spend just as much time lowering as you spend lifting.
- Engage your chest and shoulders.
- Gaze forward.

Avoid

- Feeling a sense of collapse in your chest and shoulders.
- Hunching your shoulders.
- Moving in a jerky manner.
- Taking on too much weight at once.
- Arching your back or excessively hunching it forward.
- Performing this exercise if you experience lower-back pain.

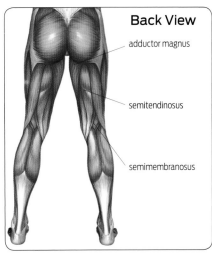

Back View

adductor magnus

semitendinosus

semimembranosus

Level
- Intermediate

Duration
- 1–3 minutes

Benefits
- Strengthens and tones core and arm muscles
- Helps to build muscle mass

Caution
- Back pain
- Knee issues

Annotation Key
* indicates deep muscles

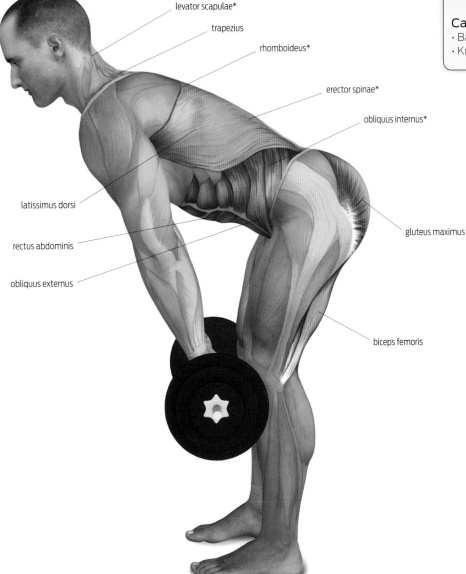

levator scapulae*

trapezius

rhomboideus*

erector spinae*

obliquus internus*

latissimus dorsi

rectus abdominis

obliquus externus

gluteus maximus

biceps femoris

Roll-Up Triceps Lift

More an exercise in deep muscle control, than one to build bulk, the Roll-Up Triceps Lift can, nevertheless, increase muscle in the core and triceps. Lifting and lowering the body while extending the arms while holding a weight is an excellent challenge for the core.

1 Lie on the floor, with your spine in a neutral position. Hold a body bar in both hands. Bend your elbows so that your arms form a right angle with the body bar above your head.

2 Keeping the rest of your body in place, straighten your arms.

Correct form
- Keep the rest of your body stable as you move smoothly and with control.
- Strongly engage your abdominal muscles as you roll up and down.
- Spend as much time rolling down as you spend rolling up.
- Focus on form over number of repetitions.
- As much as possible, keep both legs anchored to the floor.

Avoid
- Moving in a jerky manner.
- Twisting your torso or moving your hips off the floor.

3 Maintaining this arm position, use your core muscles to smoothly roll up to a sitting position. Keep your arms extended, with the body bar lifted overhead.

4 Slowly roll back to lie in the starting position. Repeat, completing 10 repetitions.

Level
· Intermediate

Duration
· 1–3 minutes

Benefits
· Strengthens and tones core muscles and triceps

Caution
· Lower-back issues
· Shoulder pain

Annotation Key
indicates deep muscles

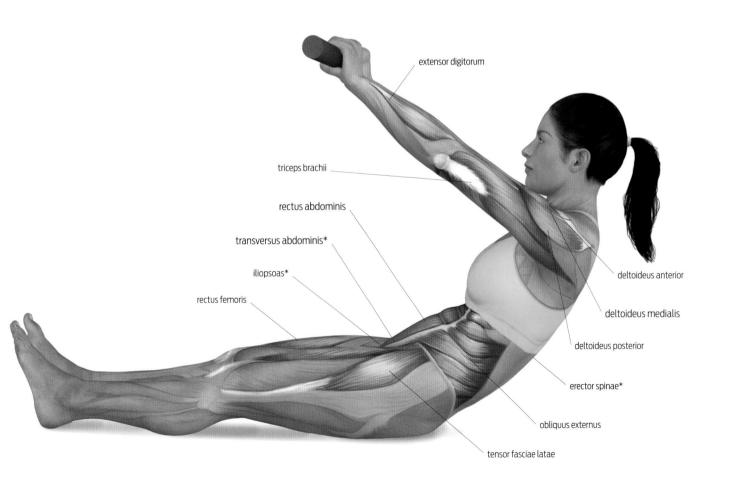

extensor digitorum

triceps brachii

rectus abdominis

transversus abdominis*

iliopsoas*

rectus femoris

deltoideus anterior

deltoideus medialis

deltoideus posterior

erector spinae*

obliquus externus

tensor fasciae latae

Lying Abduction

This exercise works both the inner and outer leg muscles. Lifting the dumbbell increases the work and will tone the upper arms, too. Stability is provided by a strong core.

1 Lie on your side, with one leg stacked on top of the other and one arm supporting you, forearm on the floor and palm down. Extend the other arm along the side of your body, a dumbbell in your hand.

2 Maintaining the position of the rest of your body, smoothly raise the top leg. Allow your top arm to rise slightly, too. If desired, hold for a few seconds.

3 Lower to starting position. Repeat, performing 10 repetitions before switching sides and repeating.

Correct form
· Gaze forward.
· Keep your legs extended.
· Lower your leg just as smoothly as you lift it.
· Keep your torso facing forward.
· Anchor your bottom arm and leg to the floor.

Avoid
·Tilting or twisting your hips as you raise your leg.
· Tensing or twisting your neck.
· Hunching your shoulders.

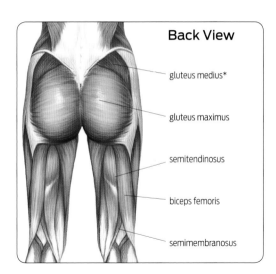

Back View

gluteus medius*

gluteus maximus

semitendinosus

biceps femoris

semimembranosus

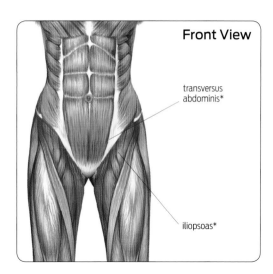

Front View

transversus abdominis*

iliopsoas*

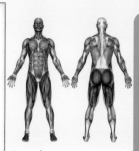

Level
· Intermediate

Duration
· 2–3 minutes

Benefits
· Strengthens and
  tones legs, arms,
  and core
· Improves balance

Caution
· Lower-back issues

Annotation Key
*indicates deep muscles

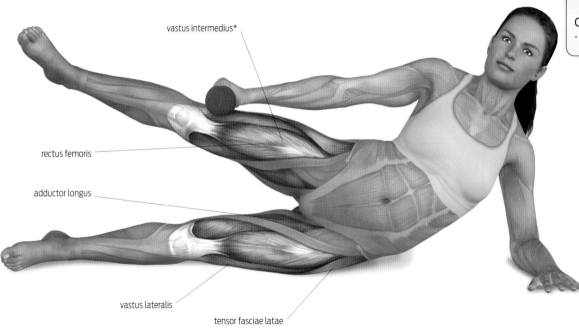

vastus intermedius*

rectus femoris

adductor longus

vastus lateralis

tensor fasciae latae

Modification

Harder: Try moving into a
side plank position. Focus on
keeping your body in a straight
line as you hold.

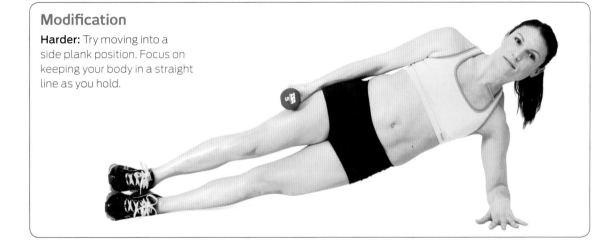

Seated Russian Twist

Adding weight to the Seated Russian Twist increases the work done by the core and upper arms. In particular, this exercise tones and strengthens the obliques, lower back extensors, and all the abdominal muscles.

Correct form
· Engage your core.
· Anchor your heels to the floor.
· Move smoothly.

Avoid
· Arching or rounding your back.
· Hunching your shoulders.
· Swinging your arms or moving in a jerky manner.
· Allowing your heels to lift off the floor.
· Tensing your neck as you twist.

1 Holding a dumbbell in both hands, sit with your legs extended in front of you, knees bent and feet about hip-width apart. Lean back slightly.

3 Bring the dumbbell to the middle of your body and then to the right side. Repeat, performing 20 rotations.

2 Engage your core muscles as you bring the dumbbell to the left side.

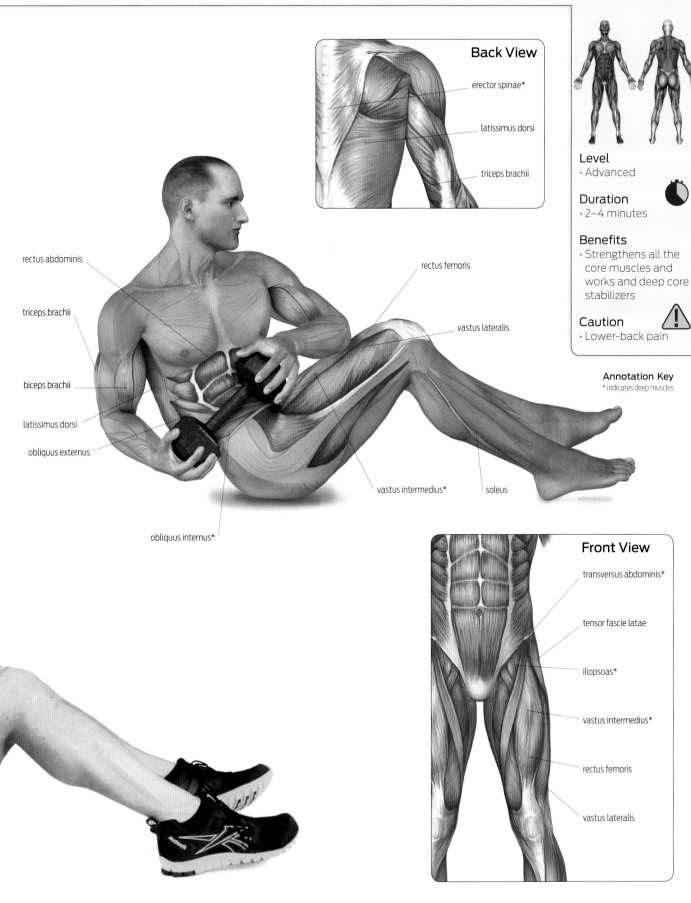

Back View

erector spinae*

latissimus dorsi

triceps brachii

Level
· Advanced

Duration
· 2–4 minutes

Benefits
· Strengthens all the core muscles and works and deep core stabilizers

Caution
· Lower-back pain

Annotation Key
* indicates deep muscles

rectus abdominis

triceps brachii

biceps brachii

latissimus dorsi

obliquus externus

obliquus internus*

rectus femoris

vastus lateralis

vastus intermedius*

soleus

Front View

transversus abdominis*

tensor fascie latae

iliopsoas*

vastus intermedius*

rectus femoris

vastus lateralis

Swiss Ball Pullover

The challenge with this exercise is to keep the body long, straight, and balanced on the Swiss ball while lifting the weight upward. The trick to doing it well is strong engagement of the core.

Correct form
· Keep your torso stable.
· Anchor both feet to the floor.
· Engage your abdominal muscles.
· Keep your buttocks and pelvis lifted so that your upper legs, torso and neck form a line.
· Lower your arms just as smoothly as you raise them.

Avoid
· Locking your arms when they are extended behind your head.
· Arching your back.
· Rushing through the exercise.
· Rolling excessively on the ball.

1 Lie face-up on the Swiss ball, with your upper back and neck supported. Extend your body, legs bent with knees directly over ankles, and feet planted on the floor slightly more than shoulder-distance apart. Using both hands, grasp a dumbbell and extend your arms behind you, level with your shoulders so that your body from knees to fingertips forms a long straight line.

2 Keeping the rest of your body stable and your arms as straight as possible, raise your arms upward.

3 Continue raising your arms until they are fully extended perpendicular to your torso.

4 Smoothly and with control, lower your arms to the starting position. Repeat, completing 15 repetitions.

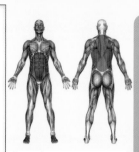

Level
· Intermediate

Duration

· 1–2 minutes

Benefits
· Stabilizes core muscles
· Strengthens and tones shoulders and upper back

Caution
· Lower-back pain
· Shoulder issues

Annotation Key
indicates deep muscles

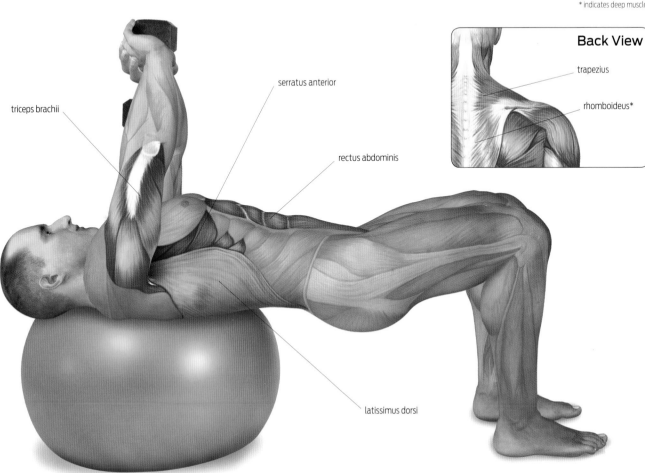

triceps brachii

serratus anterior

rectus abdominis

latissimus dorsi

Back View

trapezius

rhomboideus*

Ball Squat with Biceps Curl

Coordinating the movement of arms and legs is just one aspect of this Squat. Aim to have your knees at a 90-degree angle and to keep your upper body strong and straight.

1 Stand at a wall, with the Swiss ball against your back, grasping a dumbbell in each hand. Plant your feet slightly in front of your torso to prepare.

Correct form
· Engage your core muscles; your abs should be driving the movement.
· Keep your hips facing forward.
· Gaze forward.
· Maintain the line of your torso as you squat and rise to stand.

Avoid
· Rushing through the movement.
· Losing control of the ball.
· Twisting your hips to either side.

2 Bend your knees and lower toward the floor while curling the dumbbells toward your chest. As you lower into the squat position, keep the Swiss ball behind your back.

3 Gradually straighten your arms and legs as you rise to stand and release the dumbbells to your sides. Repeat, carrying out 15 repetitions.

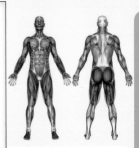

Back View

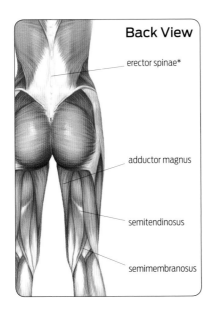

- erector spinae*
- adductor magnus
- semitendinosus
- semimembranosus

Modification

Harder: While in the squatting and curling position, extend one leg, hold and release. Repeat on the other side.

Level
· Intermediate

Duration
· 1–2 minutes

Benefits
· Strengthens and tones legs, biceps, shoulders, core, and gluteal muscles

Caution ⚠
· Lower-back pain
· Knee or ankle issues

Annotation Key
* indicates deep muscles

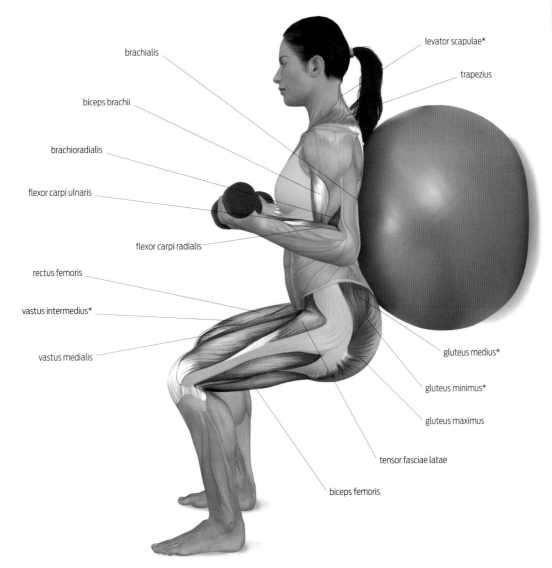

- brachialis
- biceps brachii
- brachioradialis
- flexor carpi ulnaris
- flexor carpi radialis
- rectus femoris
- vastus intermedius*
- vastus medialis
- levator scapulae*
- trapezius
- gluteus medius*
- gluteus minimus*
- gluteus maximus
- tensor fasciae latae
- biceps femoris

Lateral Step and Curl

An exercise that you might combine with Curling Step-and-Raise (pages 74–75), this focuses on the legs and biceps, along with working on your balance and agility. Work at a steady speed in order to achieve maximum workout and develop your muscle tone.

1 Stand with your feet hip-width apart and your arms at your sides, a dumbbell in each hand. Position a step beside your right foot.

2 Step to the right, placing your right foot on the step. Simultaneously bend your elbows, curling the dumbbells into your chest.

3 Lowering the dumbbells, bring your left leg onto the step.

4 Curl the dumbbells into your chest as you step your right leg off of the step. Release the dumbbells as you step down with your left leg. You should now be in the starting position with the step to your right.

Correct form
- Keep your upper arms stationary as you curl and release.
- Keep your movements smooth and controlled.
- Keep your torso facing forward.
- Pull your abdominal muscles inward.
- Gaze forward.
- Press your shoulders away from your ears.

Avoid
- Twisting your neck.
- Hunching your shoulders.
- Arching your back or hunching forward.
- Moving so quickly that you sacrifice form.

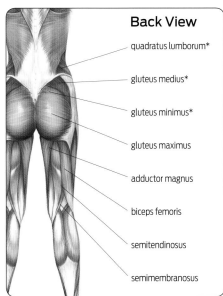

Back View

- quadratus lumborum*
- gluteus medius*
- gluteus minimus*
- gluteus maximus
- adductor magnus
- biceps femoris
- semitendinosus
- semimembranosus

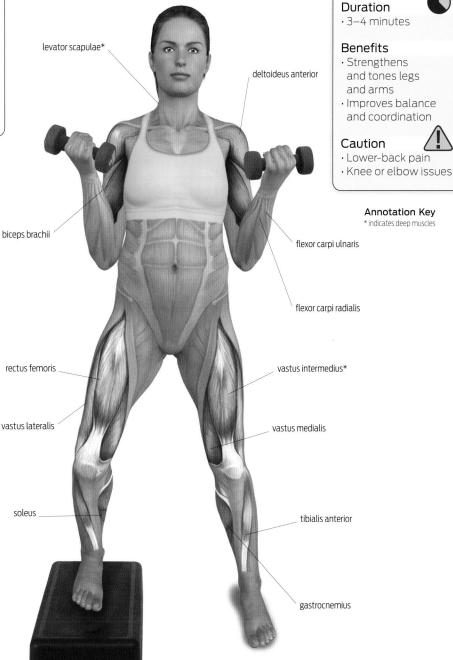

- levator scapulae*
- deltoideus anterior
- biceps brachii
- flexor carpi ulnaris
- flexor carpi radialis
- rectus femoris
- vastus intermedius*
- vastus lateralis
- vastus medialis
- soleus
- tibialis anterior
- gastrocnemius

Level
· Intermediate

Duration
· 3–4 minutes

Benefits
· Strengthens and tones legs and arms
· Improves balance and coordination

Caution
· Lower-back pain
· Knee or elbow issues

Annotation Key
* indicates deep muscles

5 Repeat, stepping to the left this time. Keeping a steady pace, complete 20 repetitions.

Crossover Step-Up

The crossover movements of this exercise work the inner and outer thighs, the hip flexors, and the lower-abdominal muscles. The effort required to maintain your balance works the rest of the core and tests your agility.

Correct form
- Keep holding the Medicine ball in front of your chest.
- Maintain a steady pace.
- Keep your torso facing forward.
- Pull your abdominal muscles inward.
- Gaze forward.
- Press your shoulders away from your ears.

Avoid
- Twisting your neck.
- Hunching your shoulders.
- Arching your back or hunching forward.
- Moving so quickly that you sacrifice form.

1 Stand with your feet hip-width apart, holding a Medicine ball in front of your chest. Position a high step and a lower step beside your left foot.

2 Cross your right leg over your left, resting it on the step. Shift weight onto the right foot to step up.

3 Rest your left foot on the lower step.

4 Again cross your right leg over your left to step down onto the floor.

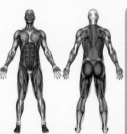

Back View

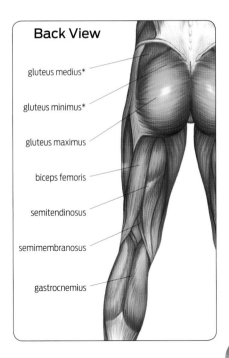

- gluteus medius*
- gluteus minimus*
- gluteus maximus
- biceps femoris
- semitendinosus
- semimembranosus
- gastrocnemius

5 Step your right leg onto the floor so that you are standing to the left of the step.

6 Repeat in the other direction. Perform 15 repetitions.

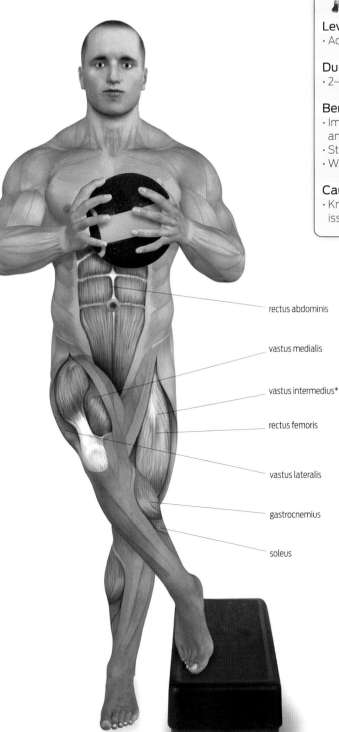

Level
· Advanced

Duration
· 2–3 minutes

Benefits
· Improves balance and coordination
· Stabilizes core
· Works legs

Caution
· Knee and ankle issues

Annotation Key
* indicates deep muscles

- rectus abdominis
- vastus medialis
- vastus intermedius*
- rectus femoris
- vastus lateralis
- gastrocnemius
- soleus

Obstacle Challenge

Coordination, balance, and agility are required for this exercise. If done fast enough and with enough repetitions, it will give an aerobic workout, but do not sacrifice form for speed. Remember to keep the Medicine ball in the same position throughout.

1 Set up a series of cones, shorter objects and a step on the floor as shown. Hold a Medicine ball in front of your chest.

2 Jump between the objects as you make your way diagonally from one corner to the other.

3 Jump over one cone and then the other.

Correct form
- Keep the Medicine ball in place and centered in front of your chest.
- Engage your abdominal muscles.
- Maintain a steady pace.

Avoid
- Twisting your neck.
- Hunching your shoulders.
- Moving in a jerky manner.
- Letting go of the ball.

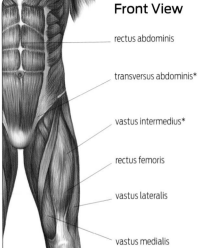

4 Still holding the ball, challenge yourself to jump over the step.

5 Jog back from the step to the beginning of the course. Begin again, completing the course up to 10 times.

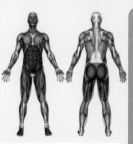

Level
· Beginner

Duration
· 5–6 minutes

Benefits
· Improves balance and coordination
· Stabilizes core

Caution
· Lower-back pain
· Knee and ankle issues

Annotation Key
* indicates deep muscles

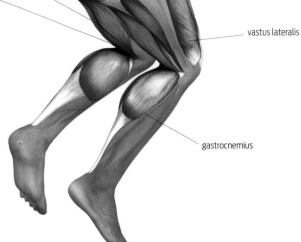

gluteus medius*

gluteus minimius*

gluteus maximus

semitendinosus

biceps femoris

semimembranosus

vastus intermedius*

rectus femoris

vastus lateralis

gastrocnemius

Front View

rectus abdominis

transversus abdominis*

vastus intermedius*

rectus femoris

vastus lateralis

vastus medialis

Contents

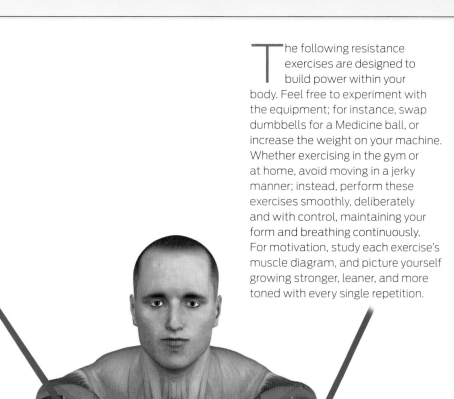

The following resistance exercises are designed to build power within your body. Feel free to experiment with the equipment; for instance, swap dumbbells for a Medicine ball, or increase the weight on your machine. Whether exercising in the gym or at home, avoid moving in a jerky manner; instead, perform these exercises smoothly, deliberately and with control, maintaining your form and breathing continuously. For motivation, study each exercise's muscle diagram, and picture yourself growing stronger, leaner, and more toned with every single repetition.

Resistance Exercises

Woodchop

Targeting the abdominal muscles and the obliques, the Woodchop is a great upper-body workout done using a cable machine. Increase the intensity of the workout by increasing the weight on the machine, but always maintain your form. Keep your gaze soft.

1 Stand with your feet slightly wider than hip-distance part, with the weight machine to your right. Grasp the handle of the cable in both hands. Your legs may be slightly bent.

2 Slowly and smoothly, rotate your core and raise your arms diagonally to the upper right, toward the cable machine.

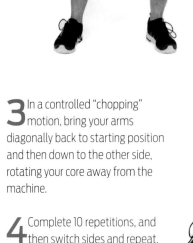

Correct form
· Move slowly and with control.
· Follow your arms with your gaze as you raise and lower.
· Keep your core contracted and your abs engaged.
· You can also perform this exercise with a resistance band, anchoring one end beneath one foot, holding the other end in both hands, and twisting in the opposite direction.

Avoid
· Locking your knees.
· Hunching your shoulders.
· Twisting your neck.
· Moving in a jerky manner from side to side.
· Raising your arms so high that you lose control of your core and/or arch your back.

3 In a controlled "chopping" motion, bring your arms diagonally back to starting position and then down to the other side, rotating your core away from the machine.

4 Complete 10 repetitions, and then switch sides and repeat.

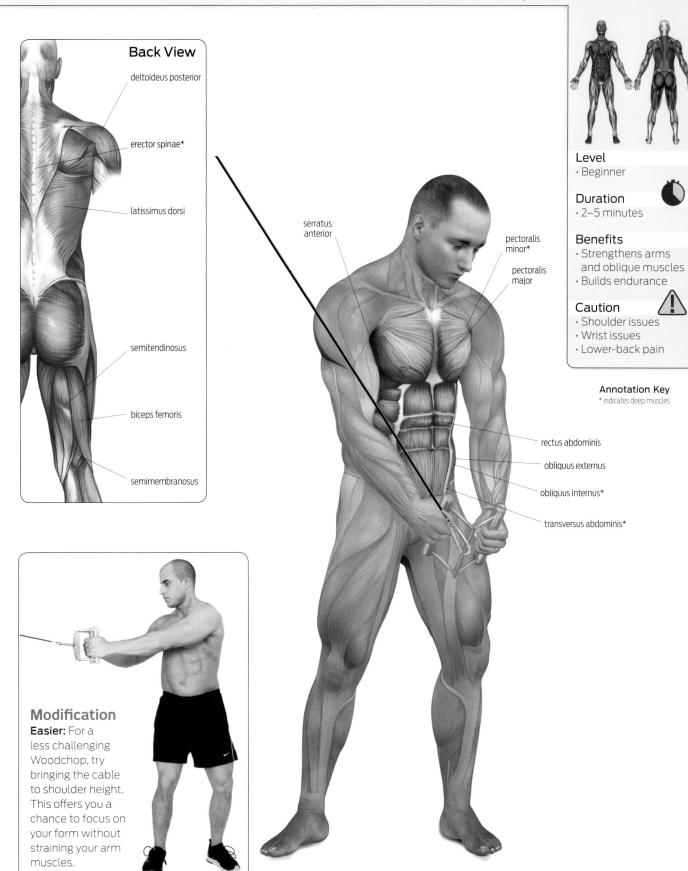

Back View

deltoideus posterior

erector spinae*

latissimus dorsi

semitendinosus

biceps femoris

semimembranosus

serratus anterior

pectoralis minor*

pectoralis major

rectus abdominis

obliquus externus

obliquus internus*

transversus abdominis*

Level
· Beginner

Duration
· 2–5 minutes

Benefits
· Strengthens arms and oblique muscles
· Builds endurance

Caution
· Shoulder issues
· Wrist issues
· Lower-back pain

Annotation Key
* indicates deep muscles

Modification
Easier: For a less challenging Woodchop, try bringing the cable to shoulder height. This offers you a chance to focus on your form without straining your arm muscles.

Twisting Lift

An excellent exercise to combine with the Woodchop (pages 100–101), the Twisting Lift also makes use of the resistance opportunities offered by a cable machine. Increase the amount of weight you use as your strength and tone increase.

1 Stand upright, facing a cable machine, with your feet planted hip-distance apart or slightly wider. Hold the cable in both hands.

Correct form
- Keep your feet planted and your torso stable as you move.
- Move slowly and with control.
- Keep your abdominal and gluteal muscles engaged throughout.

Avoid
- Moving in a jerky manner.
- Locking your knees.
- Arching your back or slumping forward.

2 In a smooth movement, pull the cable toward your body, bending your elbows to bring the cable in close to your chest. Your elbows should be almost at shoulder height.

3 Using your hips as a hinge, turn to the right side. Your arms should stay in place. Allow your left knee to bend slightly if desired.

4 Gradually twist back to starting position, facing the machine.

5 Straighten your arms, releasing the cable to return to starting position. Switch sides and repeat, aiming for 20 per side.

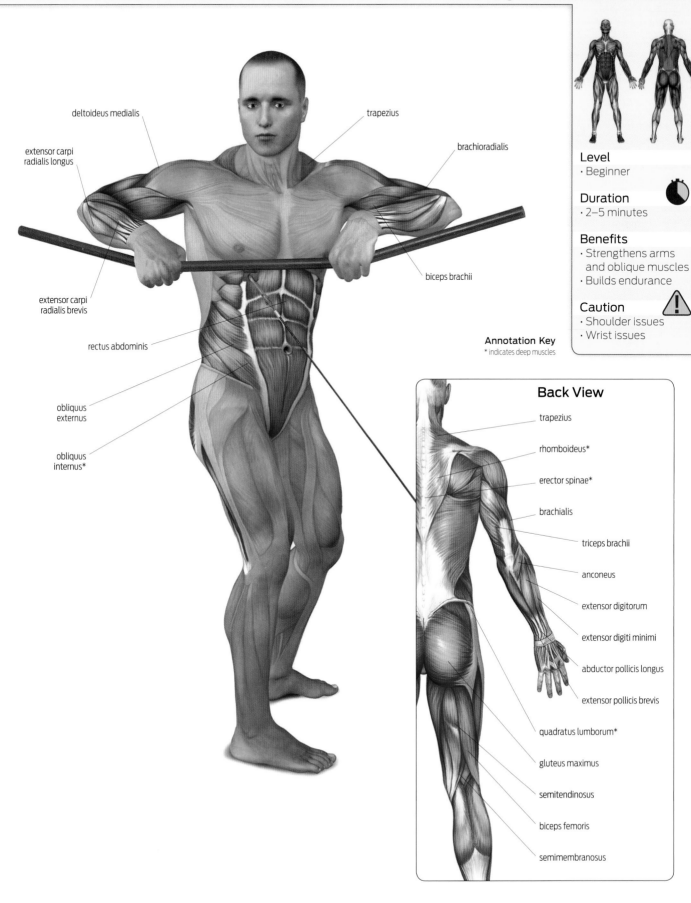

deltoideus medialis

extensor carpi
radialis longus

extensor carpi
radialis brevis

rectus abdominis

obliquus
externus

obliquus
internus*

trapezius

brachioradialis

biceps brachii

Level
· Beginner

Duration
· 2–5 minutes

Benefits
· Strengthens arms
  and oblique muscles
· Builds endurance

Caution
· Shoulder issues
· Wrist issues

Annotation Key
* indicates deep muscles

Back View

trapezius

rhomboideus*

erector spinae*

brachialis

triceps brachii

anconeus

extensor digitorum

extensor digiti minimi

abductor pollicis longus

extensor pollicis brevis

quadratus lumborum*

gluteus maximus

semitendinosus

biceps femoris

semimembranosus

Squat and Row

Creating a combination of upper and lower body work, the Squat and Row demands balance and attention to form, along with muscle control.

1 Loop a resistance band around something secure, such as a piece of gym equipment. Stand upright, holding the ends of the band. Plant your feet hip-width apart. Gaze forward.

2 In a smooth movement, begin to bend your knees. At the same time, bend your elbows as you pull both ends of the band in toward your body.

3 Keeping the rest of your body stable and your abdominal muscles engaged, use both hands to pull the band even further toward your body.

4 Smoothly return to starting position. Repeat, starting with 10 repetitions and building up to 20.

Correct form
· Keep both feet anchored to the ground.
· When bending, aim for your legs to form a right angle.
· Move slowly and with control.
· Keep your belly pulled inward.

Avoid
· Twisting your torso.
· Arching your back.
· Rushing through the movement.
· Twisting your neck to either side.
· Lowering your chin.

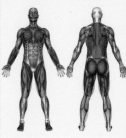

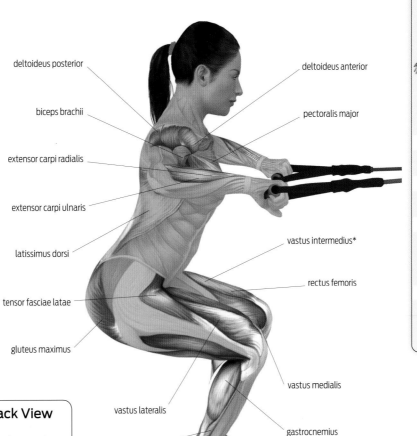

deltoideus posterior

deltoideus anterior

biceps brachii

pectoralis major

extensor carpi radialis

extensor carpi ulnaris

vastus intermedius*

latissimus dorsi

rectus femoris

tensor fasciae latae

gluteus maximus

vastus medialis

vastus lateralis

gastrocnemius

soleus

Level
· Intermediate

Duration
· 2–5 minutes

Benefits
· Strengthens legs, glutes, and shoulders
· Builds endurance

Caution
· Knee issues
· Lower-back pain
· Shoulder issues

Annotation Key
* indicates deep muscles

Back View

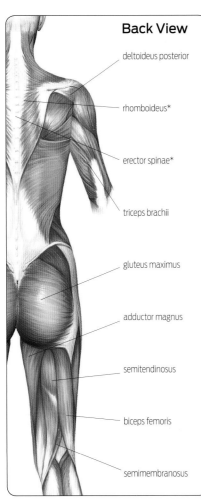

deltoideus posterior

rhomboideus*

erector spinae*

triceps brachii

gluteus maximus

adductor magnus

semitendinosus

biceps femoris

semimembranosus

Modification

Harder: Try bending one leg behind you to form a split squat while holding the cable taut. Maintain a neutral back through the exercise.

1

2

Reverse Lunge with Chest Press

This exercise can be done with resistance bands or two cable machines. If the latter, start with a lighter weight and increase it as your strength increases. Use a strong hammer grip for lower arm power.

1 Stand upright with your feet roughly hip-width apart. Grasp the handle of one resistance band in each hand. Loop the other handles of both bands around weight machines or other stable objects to either side of you. Raise your arms to hold both bands perpendicular to your body, slightly taut.

Correct form
· Keep your torso facing forward.
· Engage your abdominal and gluteal muscles.
· Move slowly and with control.

Avoid
· Twisting your torso in either direction.
· Hunching your shoulders.

2 Step your right leg behind you.

3 Bend both knees into a reverse lunge position. At the same time lower both arms, feeling resistance on the bands.

4 Gradually straighten your legs, and raise your arms to your sides to return to starting position.

5 Step your right leg forward, and repeat on the other side. Alternating, aim for 10 repetitions on each side.

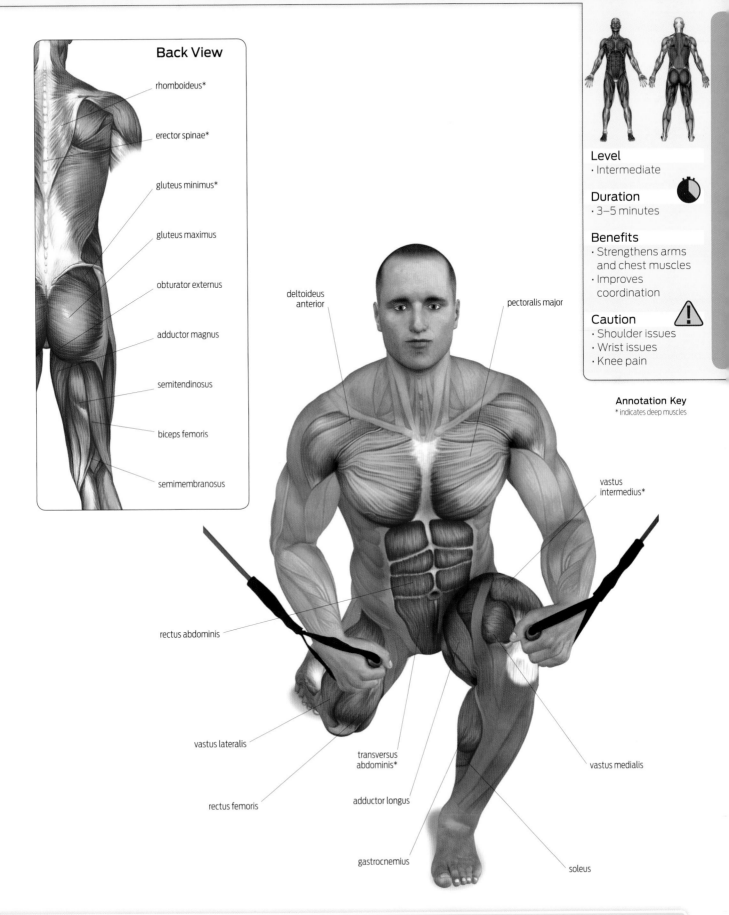

Back View

rhomboideus*

erector spinae*

gluteus minimus*

gluteus maximus

obturator externus

adductor magnus

semitendinosus

biceps femoris

semimembranosus

deltoideus anterior

pectoralis major

Level
· Intermediate

Duration
· 3–5 minutes

Benefits
· Strengthens arms and chest muscles
· Improves coordination

Caution
· Shoulder issues
· Wrist issues
· Knee pain

Annotation Key
* indicates deep muscles

vastus intermedius*

rectus abdominis

vastus lateralis

transversus abdominis*

vastus medialis

rectus femoris

adductor longus

gastrocnemius

soleus

Press and Squat

A strong coordinated movement is needed to gain the most benefit from this powerful workout. A soft forward gaze will help you to keep your form correct.

1 Loop a resistance band around a weight machine. Stand facing away from the machine, your feet planted hip-distance apart or slightly wider, and grasp one handle in each hand.

2 Bend your elbows, feeling resistance from the band as you raise both handles to shoulder height.

Correct form
· Keep your shoulders pressed down your back.
· Anchor both feet to the floor.
· Keep your torso facing forward and your hips level as you lift and lower.

Avoid
· Locking your knees.
· Arching your back.
· Letting your neck twist.
· Twisting your torso to either side.

3 Bend your knees into a squat position. Simultaneously straighten both arms in front of you, feeling resistance as you press.

4 Gradually straighten your knees and slowly return your arms to starting position. Perform 15 repetitions.

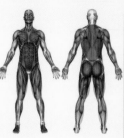

Back View

- erector spinae*
- gluteus minimus*
- gluteus maximus
- obturator externus
- adductor magnus
- semitendinosus
- biceps femoris
- semimembranosus

Level
· Advanced

Duration
· 2–3 minutes

Benefits
· Strengthens and tones arms, core, and gluteal muscles

Caution
· Wrist issues
· Lower-back pain
· Shoulder issues

Annotation Key
* indicates deep muscles

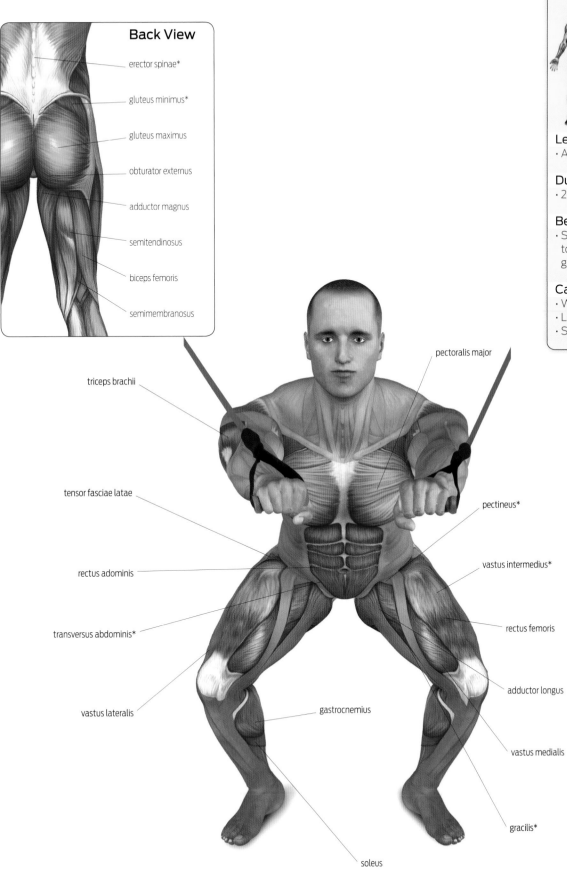

- triceps brachii
- pectoralis major
- tensor fasciae latae
- rectus adominis
- transversus abdominis*
- vastus lateralis
- gastrocnemius
- soleus
- pectineus*
- vastus intermedius*
- rectus femoris
- adductor longus
- vastus medialis
- gracilis*

Hip Extension with Reverse Fly

Calling for good balance, as well as coordination, this exercise is excellent for toning and strengthening the biceps femoris along with the quads and abs. Maintain your balance throughout; start again if you begin to wobble.

1 Stand upright, facing a cable machine, with your feet less than hip-width apart and a cable attached to your right ankle. Hold one dumbbell in each hand.

2 Begin to smoothly lift your right leg off the floor. Simultaneously, lift both arms out to your sides. Allow your torso to hinge forward slightly as you lift.

3 Continue to lift your arms and your leg, raising them as high as you can go without arching your back. Your hips should remain stable and facing forward.

4 Gradually lower your right foot to the floor, lower your arms to your sides, and stand upright to return to starting position.

5 Repeat, aiming for 5 repetitions at first. Then, switch the cable to your left ankle and repeat.

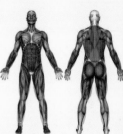

Back View

- trapezius
- deltoideus posterior
- rhomboideus*
- erector spinae*
- brachialis
- triceps brachii
- anconeus
- extensor digitorum
- extensor digiti minimi
- abductor pollicis longus
- extensor pollicis brevis
- quadratus lumborum*
- semimembranosus

Correct form
- Move both of your arms and your weighted leg at roughly the same pace.
- Gaze forward, focusing on a spot in front of you to help with balance.
- Keep your abdominal and gluteal muscles pulled in and engaged.

Avoid
- Rushing through any part of the movement.
- Twisting your hips to either side.
- Hunching your shoulders.
- Letting your neck twist.

Level
- Advanced

Duration

- 2–3 minutes

Benefits
- Strengthens and tones arms, back, and core
- Improves coordination

Caution
- Wrist issues
- Shoulder issues
- Lower-back pain

Annotation Key
* indicates deep muscles

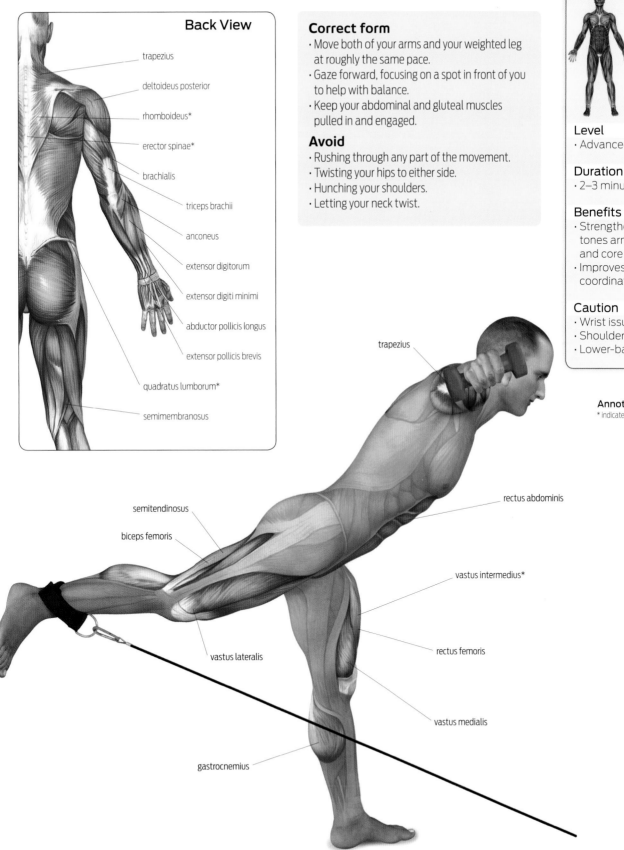

- trapezius
- rectus abdominis
- semitendinosus
- biceps femoris
- vastus intermedius*
- rectus femoris
- vastus lateralis
- vastus medialis
- gastrocnemius

Contents

Stretching and releasing your muscles is vital to your fitness regimen. The following exercises will increase your range of motion while also releasing stiffness and imbalance from poor posture or overworked muscles. If performed after a workout, these stretches will release fascia (the connective tissue surrounding the muscles), as well as the lactic acid that builds up during exercise. In addition, they will increase circulation and create a feeling of relaxation and well-being. Perform them on their own, or during or after an exercise session.

Stretching & Releasing

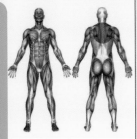

Triceps Stretch

This stretch targets the backs of the upper arms. Done correctly, it mobilizes the shoulders and works on core stablity. Keep the movement within comfortable bounds, aiming to increase the stretch over time.

Level
· Beginner

Duration
· 1½–2 minutes

Benefits
· Strengthens and tones upper arms

Caution
· Shoulder issues
· Arm issues
· Any back pain

Annotation Key
* indicates deep muscles

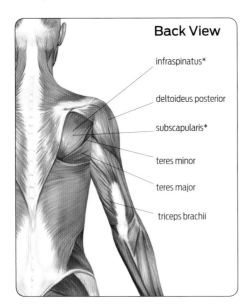

Back View

infraspinatus*

deltoideus posterior

subscapularis*

teres minor

teres major

triceps brachii

1 Stand upright, with your arms at your sides. Raise both arms over your head.

2 Begin to bend both arms. With one hand, grasp the elbow of the other arm, and gently pull.

3 Continue to pull your elbow back until you feel the stretch on the underside of your arm.

4 Hold for 15 seconds. Release, lowering your arms to your sides. Repeat on the other side. Perform 3 times on each arm.

Correct form
· Have your pelvis slightly tucked with a stable stance.
· Think about remaining upright and gently stretching the arms.

Avoid
· Tilting your head.

Pectoral Stretch

All stretches rely on slow, controlled movement. This one works the pecs, but also increases mobility in the shoulders and upper arms. A soft gaze will assist your stretch and ensure you keep it gentle.

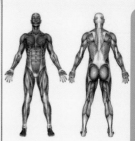

Level
· Beginner

Duration
· 1½–2 minutes

Benefits
· Stretches pecs and shoulders

Caution
· Shoulder issues
· Wrist issues
· Lower-back pain

Annotation Key
* indicates deep muscles

1 Stand upright, with your arms at your sides.

2 Bring your arms behind your back. Clasp your hands together.

3 Keeping the rest of your body still, imagine your shoulder blades moving toward one another as you lift and reach your clasped hands away from your body.

4 Hold for 15 seconds. Release, and then return to starting position. Repeat 3 times.

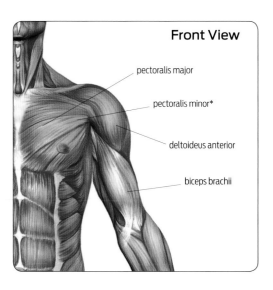

Front View

pectoralis major

pectoralis minor*

deltoideus anterior

biceps brachii

Correct form
· Keep your elbows straight as you move your arms.
· Keep your torso straight and upright.
· To intensify the stretch, try turning your palms outward while lifting your arms.
· Gaze forward.

Avoid
· Leaning your trunk too far forward.
· Turning your head to either side.
· Hunching your shoulders.
· Arching your back excessively.
· Slumping forward.

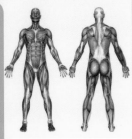

Calf Stretch

It is useful to do lower leg stretches before and during workout exercises. This stretch releases tension in the calf muscles. Concentrate on achieving a slow, deep stretch and think about your balance, too.

Level
· Beginner

Duration
· 1½–2 minutes

Benefits
· Stretches and mobilizes back of leg

Caution
· Ankle issues
· Achilles stiffness
· Lower-back pain

1 Stand with your feet parallel and shoulder-width apart. Extend your left leg forward.

2 Bend your right knee as you tip your hips slightly forward. Flex your left foot, keeping the left leg straight.

3 Hold for 15 seconds. Release, and then repeat on the other side. Perform 3 times on each leg.

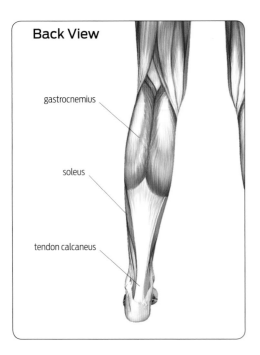

Back View

gastrocnemius

soleus

tendon calcaneus

Correct form
· To enhance the stretch, bend your knee more deeply and lower your body further.
· Keep your foot strongly flexed.

Avoid
· Tensing your shoulders.

Quadriceps Stretch

This upper leg stretch works well in tandem with the calf stretch and can be performed before and during other exercises to release tension and increase flexibility and mobility in the legs. Good balance is required; use a wall if necessary.

1 Stand with your feet together. Bend your left leg behind you, and grasp your foot with your left hand.

2 Pull your heel toward your buttocks until you feel a stretch in the front of your left thigh.

3 Hold for 15 seconds. Release, and then repeat on the other side. Perform 3 times on each leg.

Level
· Beginner

Duration
· 1½–2 minutes

Benefits
· Quads, ankles, and tops of feet

Caution
· Knee issues
· Ankle stiffness
· Lower-back pain

Annotation Key
* indicates deep muscles

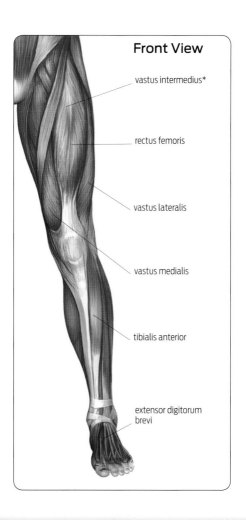

Front View

vastus intermedius*

rectus femoris

vastus lateralis

vastus medialis

tibialis anterior

extensor digitorum brevi

Correct form
· Stand upright and bring the ankle toward the buttocks, rather than the other way around.
· Keep your shoulders low and loose, your upper body straight.

Avoid
· Tensing your shoulders or forcing any part of the movement. It is better to gradually increase the depth of the stretch over time.

Piriformis Stretch

While this stretch is intended to reduce stiffness in the pelvic girdle, it will also lengthen and relax the spine. Like all stretches, it should be done slowly, smoothly and without force.

1 Lie on your back, with your legs extended and your arms along your sides. Bend your knees.

2 Keeping your arms and torso in place, lift both feet off the ground. Bring your right ankle over your left knee, resting it on the thigh.

Correct form
· Relax your hips to enable a deeper stretch.
· Keep your shoulders on the floor.

Avoid
· Pulling your thigh to your chest too forcefully, or in a jerky manner.
· Lifting your neck off the floor.

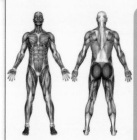

3 Grasp your left thigh with both hands. On an exhalation, gently pull your left thigh toward your chest until you feel a stretch.

4 Hold for 15 seconds. Release, and then repeat on the other side.

Level
· Beginner

Duration
· 1–2 minutes

Benefits
· Mobilizes the hips, piriformis, glutes, and lower back

Caution
· Shoulder issues
· Hip issues
· Lower-back pain

Annotation Key
* indicates deep muscles

gluteus maximus

piriformis*

gluteus minimus*

gluteus medius*

Hip-to-Thigh Stretch

Working the legs and hips, this stretch requires control and balance. When you first try it, reduce the amount of forward press. Never force the movement or compromise your balance.

1 Kneeling on your right knee, place your left foot in front of you. Your left foot should be flat on the floor, your right heel lifted.

2 Shift your weight, and gradually bring your torso forward, bending your left knee more deeply so that the knee shifts toward your toes.

Correct form
· Relax your shoulders and neck.
· Keep your upper body stable.

Avoid
· Performing this exercise if you have groin injury.

3 Keeping your torso stable, press your left hip forward until you feel a stretch over the front of your thigh.

4 Raise your arms toward the ceiling. Hold for 10 seconds, release, and repeat up to 4 more times. Switch sides, and repeat.

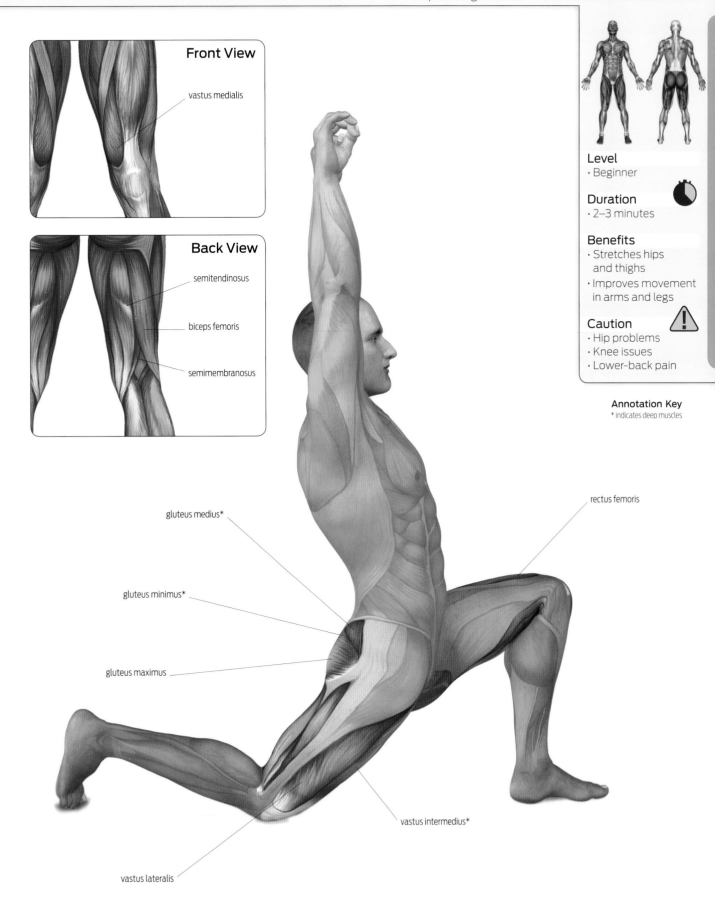

Front View

vastus medialis

Back View

semitendinosus

biceps femoris

semimembranosus

Level
· Beginner

Duration
· 2–3 minutes

Benefits
· Stretches hips and thighs
· Improves movement in arms and legs

Caution
· Hip problems
· Knee issues
· Lower-back pain

Annotation Key
* indicates deep muscles

gluteus medius*

gluteus minimus*

gluteus maximus

rectus femoris

vastus intermedius*

vastus lateralis

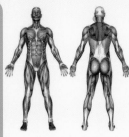

Neck Flexion

Along with the shoulders, necks are often tense and stiff. Neck stretches, such as this one and the one opposite, can be done regularly to ease tightness and mobilize the muscles of the upper body.

Level
· Beginner

Duration
· 1½–2 minutes

Benefits
· Loosens the neck and shoulders

Caution
· Neck issues
· Shoulder stiffness
· Upper-back pain

Annotation Key
*indicates deep muscles

1 Stand upright. Place one hand on your head. Gradually pull your chin toward your chest until you feel a stretch in the back of your neck.

2 Hold for 15 seconds. Release, and then repeat 2 more times. Switch sides, and repeat.

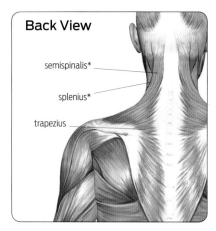

Back View

semispinalis*

splenius*

trapezius

Correct form
· Keep one arm at your side.
· Let your gaze fall forward.
· Stretch gently.
· Keep your back straight.

Avoid
· Hunching your shoulders.
· Pulling your head forward so forcefully that the stretch feels uncomfortable.

Neck Side Bend

Easing and releasing the top of the shoulders and the neck muscles, this stretch should be done slowly and gently. Avoid forcing any part of the movement, instead proceed slowly and feel each muscle releasing.

1 Stand upright. Gently grasp the side of your head with one hand.

2 Reach toward the small of the back with your other hand, bending your arm at the elbow.

3 Tilt your head toward your raised elbow until you feel a stretch in the side of your neck.

4 Hold for 15 seconds. Release, and then repeat 2 more times. Switch sides, and repeat.

Level
· Beginner

Duration
· 1½–2 minutes

Benefits
· Releases stiffness in sides of neck

Caution
· Shoulder issues
· Wrist issues
· Neck or back pain

Annotation Key
* indicates deep muscles

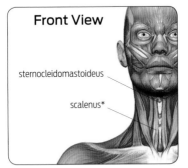

Front View

sternocleidomastoideus

scalenus*

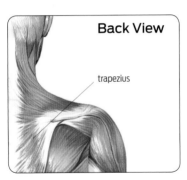

Back View

trapezius

Correct form
· Stand softly upright with the legs slightly apart.
· Keep the arms soft and loose, avoid pressing on your back.
· Keep your back straight.

Avoid
· Tensing your shoulders.
· Pulling your head into position. Keep the stretch comfortable.

Iliotibial Band Stretch

Targeting the strong fibrous tissue that surrounds the hips and connects with the knees, this stretch will increase hip mobility. It may also help protect the knee joints, which rely on this tissue for stability.

1 Stand upright, with your arms along your sides. Cross one foot in front of the other.

2 Bending at your waist, gradually reach toward the floor with your hands.

3 Hold for 15 seconds. Release, slowly roll up and repeat twice. Switch sides, and repeat.

Correct form
· Keep your knees straight (yet soft) throughout the exercise.
· Let your head drop slowly.

Avoid
· Bending or locking your knees.
· Twisting your neck, shoulders or torso to either side.

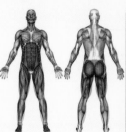

Modification

Easier: If you find it difficult to reach the floor with your hands while maintaining your form, hold the stretch when your hands are only partway to the floor. Try to reach slightly lower each time you do the stretch.

Level
· Beginner

Duration
· 1½–2 minutes

Benefits
· Stretches IT band
· Counteracts effects of wearing high heels

Caution
· Neck issues
· Hip or knee issues
· Lower-back pain

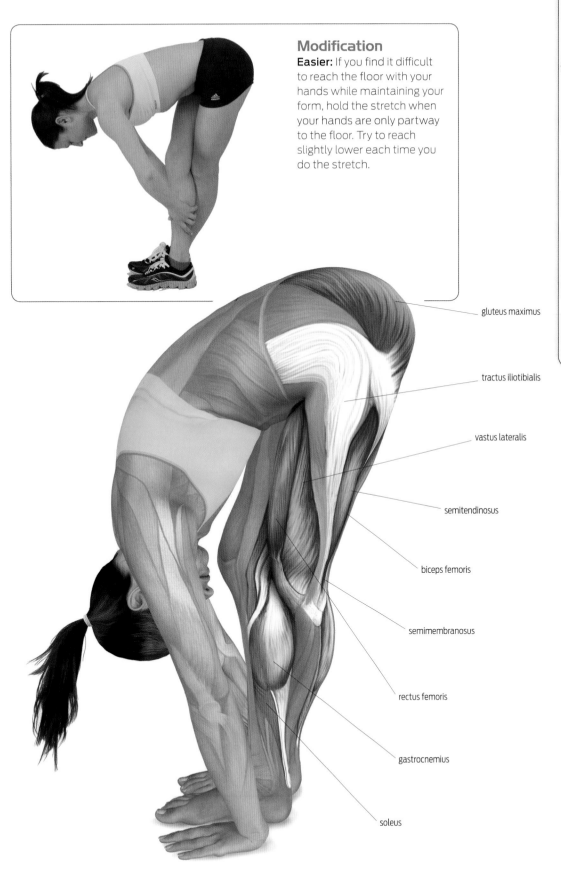

gluteus maximus

tractus iliotibialis

vastus lateralis

semitendinosus

biceps femoris

semimembranosus

rectus femoris

gastrocnemius

soleus

Supine Hamstrings Stretch

Increasing leg flexibility is one of the benefits of this deep hamstring stretch. As you practise, you can increase the stretch by keeping the lower leg straight. Use your core to help lift your leg; keep your back firmly on the ground.

1 Lie on your back with both knees bent and your feet flat on the floor.

2 Using both hands, grasp one leg just above the knee.

3 Gradually draw your knee toward your chest.

4 Keeping your knee in place, begin to straighten your leg. Your toe should be flexed.

5 Release your leg into the stretch. Maintaining your form, pull your leg toward your chest.

6 Let go of your leg, return to starting position, and repeat on the other side. Perform up to 10 times per leg.

Correct form
· Contract your quadriceps as you begin to straighten your leg.
· Keep the foot of your lower leg on the floor.
· Keep your knee pulled into your chest throughout the stretch.
· Relax your neck and shoulders.

Avoid
· Lifting your head.
· Rounding your shoulders.
· Letting your stabilizing leg shift to either side.

Modification

Harder: Straighten your lower leg so that it lies flat on the floor. Draw your other knee toward your chest. Maintain your form as you stretch.

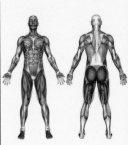

Level
· Beginner

Duration
· 1½–3½ minutes

Benefits
· Stretches hamstrings
· Helps prevent lower-back pain

Caution
· Hip injury
· Knee issues

Annotation Key
* indicates deep muscles

Back View

gluteus minimus*

semitendinosus

semimembranosus

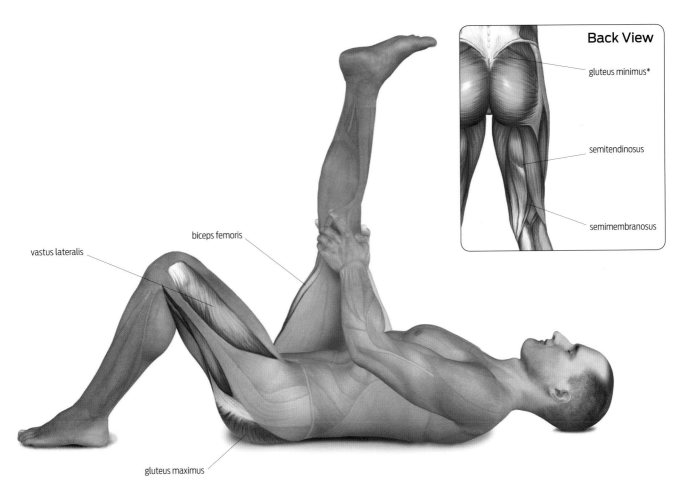

vastus lateralis

biceps femoris

gluteus maximus

Side Adductor Stretch

A key stretch to improve stability and upper leg strength and flexibility, this exercise also works all the muscles of the lower body and legs. Control of the movement is vital. Keep it slow and smooth to ensure maximum benefit.

Correct form
· Keep your spine neutral and your torso facing forward.
· Let your shoulders come slightly forward as you stretch.
· Anchor your feet to the floor.
· Gaze forward.

Avoid
· Rounding your spine.
· Hunching your shoulders and tensing your neck.
· Letting either foot lift off the floor.
· Allowing your knees to extend over your toes as you bend.

1 Stand upright. Separate your feet until they are wider than hip-distance apart, toes turned slightly outward. If desired, rest your hands just above your knees.

2 Keeping your torso steady, gradually bend your knees.

3 Without moving your torso, shift your weight to one side, bending your knee while straightening and extending your opposite leg.

4 Hold, aiming for 10 seconds. Release, return to starting position and then repeat on the other side.

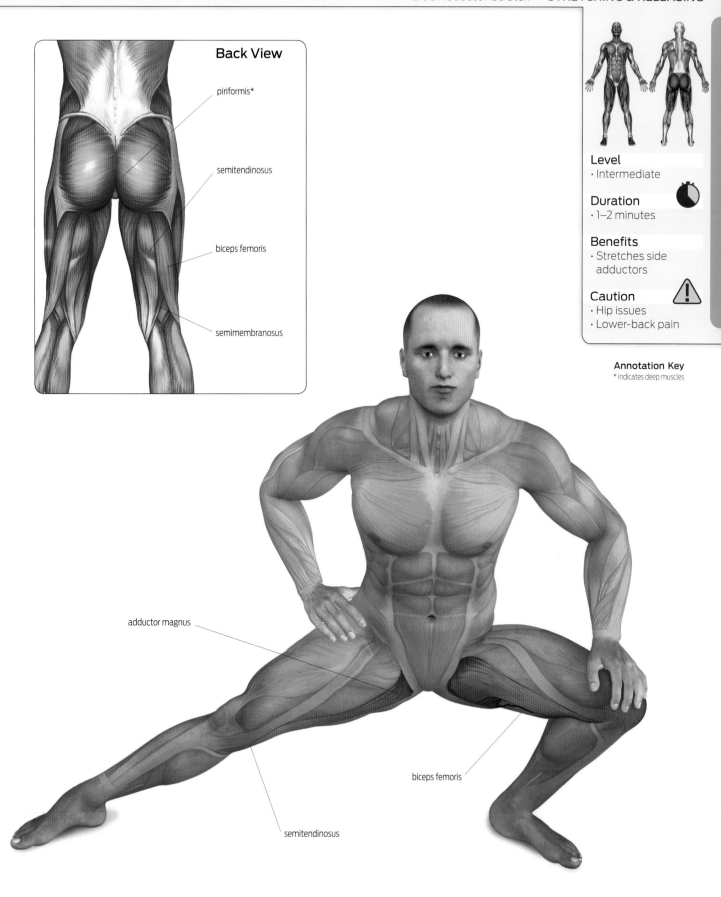

Back View

piriformis*

semitendinosus

biceps femoris

semimembranosus

Level
· Intermediate

Duration
· 1–2 minutes

Benefits
· Stretches side adductors

Caution
· Hip issues
· Lower-back pain

Annotation Key
* indicates deep muscles

adductor magnus

biceps femoris

semitendinosus

Cobra Stretch

The Cobra has its origins in yoga, but it is a good stretch for any exercise regimen and targets a number of key muscle groups, deep as well as superficial. It increases their flexibility and helps to mobilize them for an all over workout.

Correct form
· Gaze forward.
· Keep your elbows pulled in toward your body.
· Lift from your chest and back, rather than depending too much on your arms to create the arch in your back.
· Keep your shoulders and elbows pressed back.
· Press your pubic bone into the floor as you lift.

Avoid
· Tensing your buttocks.
· Splaying your elbows out to the sides.
· Lifting your hips off the floor.
· Twisting your neck.

1 Lie facedown. Bend your elbows, placing your hands flat on the floor beside your chest. Extend your legs, and press down into the floor with your thighs and the tops of your feet.

2 Inhaling, lift your chest off the floor, pressing your palms downward.

3 Continue lifting your chest as you straighten your arms, keeping your elbows soft.

4 Hold for 15 to 30 seconds. On an exhalation, lower yourself to the floor.

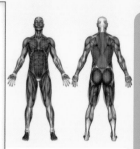

Front View

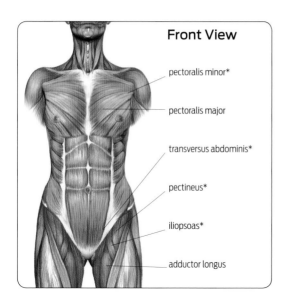

- pectoralis minor*
- pectoralis major
- transversus abdominis*
- pectineus*
- iliopsoas*
- adductor longus

Back View

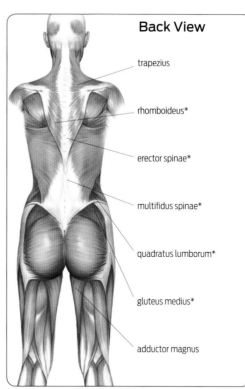

- trapezius
- rhomboideus*
- erector spinae*
- multifidus spinae*
- quadratus lumborum*
- gluteus medius*
- adductor magnus

Level
· Intermediate

Duration
· 1–2 minutes

Benefits
· Strengthens spine and gluteal muscles
· Stretches chest, abdominals and shoulders

Caution
· Back pain
· Wrist issues

Annotation Key
* indicates deep muscles

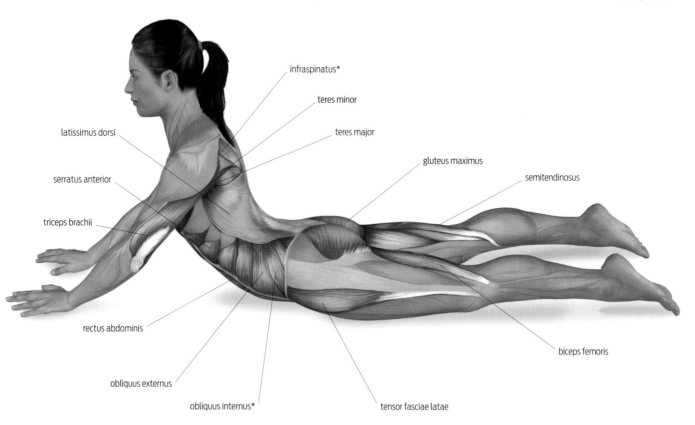

- infraspinatus*
- teres minor
- teres major
- latissimus dorsi
- serratus anterior
- triceps brachii
- gluteus maximus
- semitendinosus
- rectus abdominis
- biceps femoris
- obliquus externus
- obliquus internus*
- tensor fasciae latae

Kneeling Side Lift

Exercises that call for lifing a leg to the side are excellent for core stability as well as for working the muscles of both the raised limb and the supporting one. Balance is vital. If you feel unstable at any point, start again.

1 Kneel on the floor, with your left leg outstretched to the side and your right leg lined up under your hips. Place both hands behind your head, with your elbows pointing out to the sides.

2 Begin leaning your torso to the right.

Correct form
· Relax and lengthen your neck.
· Elongate your leg as much as possible.
· Lift your leg only as high as you can go without affecting your form.
· Keep your abs, especially the obliques, strongly engaged.

Avoid
· Twisting your torso.
· Hunching your shoulders.
· Arching your back or hunching forward.
· Tensing your neck.

3 Lift your left leg off the floor, bringing it as high as your hips.

4 Lower your leg. Repeat 3 to 5 times, and then switch sides and repeat.

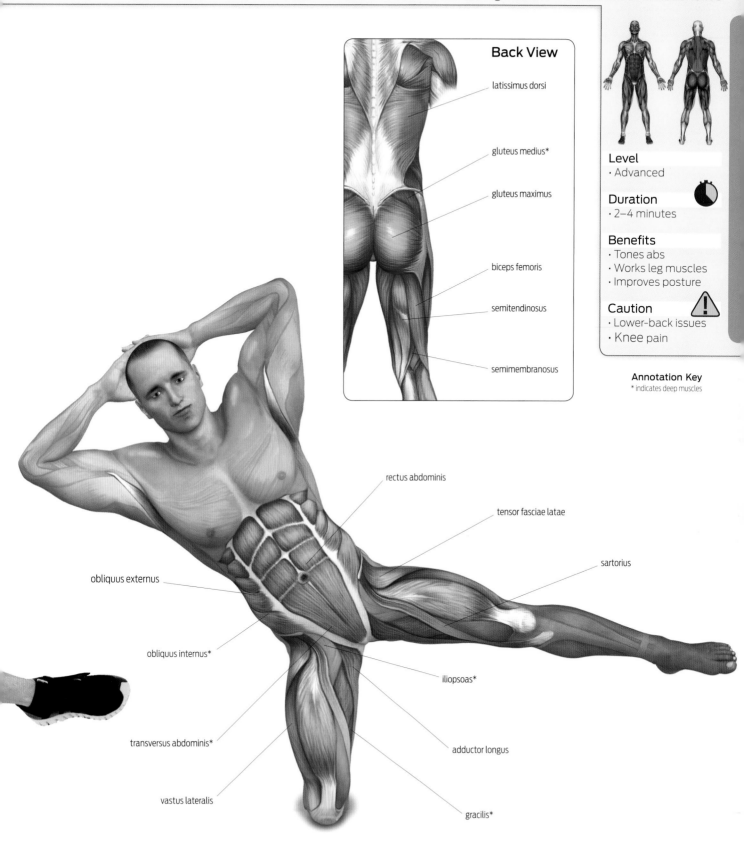

Back View

latissimus dorsi

gluteus medius*

gluteus maximus

biceps femoris

semitendinosus

semimembranosus

Level
· Advanced

Duration
· 2–4 minutes

Benefits
· Tones abs
· Works leg muscles
· Improves posture

Caution
· Lower-back issues
· Knee pain

Annotation Key
* indicates deep muscles

rectus abdominis

tensor fasciae latae

sartorius

obliquus externus

obliquus internus*

iliopsoas*

transversus abdominis*

adductor longus

vastus lateralis

gracilis*

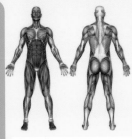

Quadriceps Roll

Using a foam roller promotes myofacial release, easing out tightness deep inside the muscles. This exercise focuses on the quads. These four hardworking muscle groups are positioned around the front of the thigh. They are key to leg strength and endurance. Ensuring they remain mobile and supple will pay great dividends in overall body fitness.

Level
· Beginner

Duration
· 1½–2 minutes

Benefits
· Strengthens and tones whole body

Caution
· Hip issues
· Shoulder issues
· Knee pain

Annotation Key
* indicates deep muscles

Correct form
· Press your palms into the floor as you roll back and forth.
· Point your toes.
· Pull in your abdominal muscles.
· Keep your palms anchored.
· Gaze towards the floor.

Avoid
· Turning your neck.
· Twisting your torso to either side.

Front View

rectus abdominus

vastus intermedius*

rectus femoris

vastus lateralis

vastus medialis

1 Kneel on the floor, with your buttocks resting on your heels. Place the foam roller just in front of your knees.

2 Raise your buttocks off your heels, and extend your body forward over the roller, palms to the floor. Extend your legs behind you so that they form a straight line.

3 Roll forward until the roller is just above your knees, and then roll back to the starting position. Repeat up to 15 times.

Hamstrings Roll

This release is ideal for doing in tandem with the Quadriceps Roll (opposite) since it works on the three hamstring muscles, positioned on the other side of the thigh. These muscles benefit from stretching before and after any workout regimen.

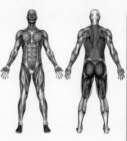

Correct form
· Press your palms into the floor.
· Keep your arms and abs strongly engaged.
· Gaze forward.
· Keep both legs extended.

Avoid
· Positioning the foam roller at your knee.
· Letting your belly bulge outward.
· Twisting your hips to either side.
· Letting your palms come off the floor.

Level
· Beginner

Duration
· 1½–2 minutes

Benefits
· Relieves tightness in hamstrings

Caution
· Hip issues
· Lower-back issues
· Hamstring pain

Annotation Key
indicates deep muscles

1 Sit on the floor, resting your palms behind you, fingers pointing forward. Position the foam roller beneath your thighs, just above the knees. Extend both legs, heels slightly off the floor.

2 Pushing forward with your arms, roll forward until the foam roller is below the uppermost part of the backs of your thighs.

3 Roll back to starting position. Repeat up to 15 times.

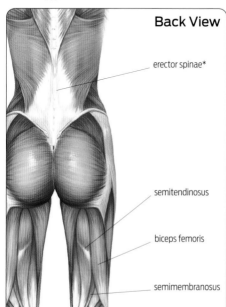

Back View

erector spinae*

semitendinosus

biceps femoris

semimembranosus

Gluteal Roll

The large, strong muscles of the buttocks are targeted during the Gluteal Roll. The exercise is ideal for those who spend a great deal of their time sitting at a desk, which can make the buttocks stiff and underworked. Make sure to include the whole buttock area and keep the movement slow and controlled.

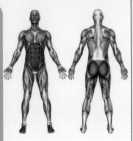

Level
· Beginner

Duration
· 1–2 minutes

Benefits
· Relieves tightness in gluteal muscles

Caution
· Shoulder pain
· Wrist issues
· Lower-back pain

Annotation Key
* indicates deep muscles

1 Sit on the floor, resting your palms on the floor behind you. Position the foam roller beneath the upper part of your buttocks. Extend both legs, resting your heels on the floor.

2 In a controlled movement, roll slightly back until the roller is beneath the lower part of your buttocks.

3 Return to the starting position. Repeat, performing up to 10 repetitions.

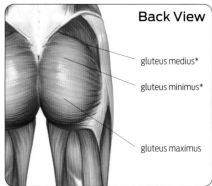

Correct form
· Gaze forward.
· Move smoothly.
· Press your palms into the floor.
· Keep your arms and abs strongly engaged.

Avoid
· Arching your back.
· Twisting your torso.
· Letting your palms come off the floor.

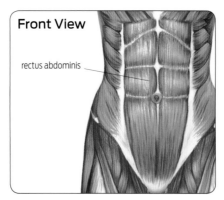

Front View

rectus abdominis

Back View

gluteus medius*

gluteus minimus*

gluteus maximus

Latissimus Roll

Most workouts include exercises for strengthening and testing the upper body, and the Latissimus Roll is perfect for stretching and releasing these muscles afterward. This exercise also works the scapular stabilizers and lateral trunk muscles, easing any stiffness.

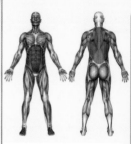

1 Lie on your right side, with the foam roller below the side of your upper chest and your legs extended. Support your torso by placing your right forearm on the floor.

2 Bend your left leg and cross it in front of your right, placing your left foot on the floor.

3 Pushing into the floor with your left leg, roll forward so that the roller moves down the side of your torso.

4 Smoothly roll back to starting position. Repeat, completing 5 repetitions. Switch sides and repeat.

Level
· Intermediate

Duration
· 1½–2 minutes

Benefits
· Relieves tightness in lats

Caution
· Lower-back pain
· Shoulder issues
· Neck stiffness

Annotation Key
* indicates deep muscles

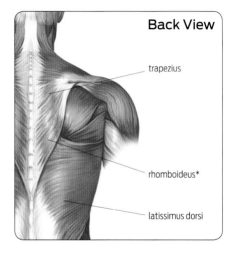

Back View

- trapezius
- rhomboideus*
- latissimus dorsi

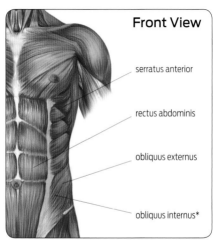

Front View

- serratus anterior
- rectus abdominis
- obliquus externus
- obliquus internus*

Correct form
· Move smoothly.
· Keep your abs engaged.
· Press your forearm into the floor.
· Press your shoulders down toward your back.
· Gaze forward.

Avoid
· Arching your back.
· Hunching your shoulders.
· Tensing your neck.

Tensor Fasciae Latae Roll

Forming part of the support structure of the pelvis, and working with the iliotibial band and the glutes, this slender thigh muscle is prone to strain during many sporting activities. Doing gentle, but deep stretches, such as this roll, can help reduce pain and tension.

1 Lie on your right side, with your legs extended so that your body forms a line. Position the foam roller beneath the side of your upper thigh.

2 Bend your left leg and cross it in front of your right leg, placing your left foot on the floor.

3 Pushing into the floor with your left leg, roll forward so that the roller moves down the side of your upper leg.

4 Smoothly roll back to starting position. Repeat, completing 5 repetitions. Switch sides and repeat.

Correct form
· Move smoothly.
· Keep your abs engaged.
· Press your palm into the floor.
· Press your shoulders down toward your back.
· Gaze forward.

Avoid
· Arching your back.
· Hunching your shoulders.
· Tensing your neck.

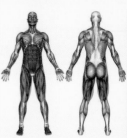

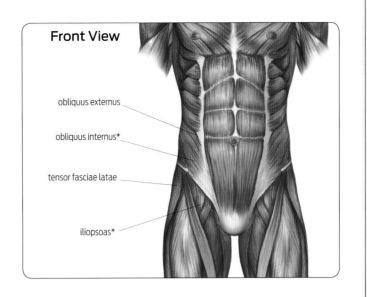

Front View

- obliquus externus
- obliquus internus*
- tensor fasciae latae
- iliopsoas*

Level
· Intermediate

Duration
· 1½–2 minutes

Benefits
· Relieves soreness in tensor fasciae latae
· Strengthens trunk

Caution
· Lower-back pain
· Pelvic injury

Annotation Key
* indicates deep muscles

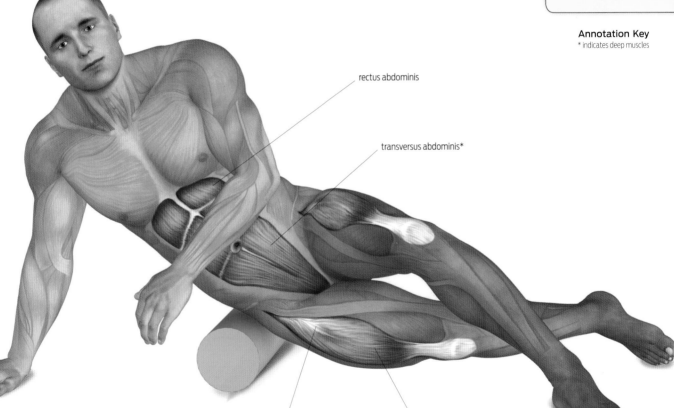

- rectus abdominis
- transversus abdominis*
- vastus intermedius*
- rectus femoris

Back Roll

Stiffness, pain, and reduced mobility are all classic back problems, made worse by a desk job or lifting heavy items. A few minutes spent stretching and easing the back muscles will reduce and relieve problems, especially if the exercise is done regularly.

1 Sit with your legs bent, extended in front of you, and your arms at your sides, palms on the floor. Position the foam roller behind you.

2 Extend your legs and lean back, engaging your core muscles as you rest your lower back on the roller.

Correct form
· Gaze forward.
· Move smoothly and with control.
· Use your arms, legs and abs to drive the movement.
· Press your palms into the floor.
· Press your shoulders down toward your back.

Avoid
· Arching your back.
· Hunching your shoulders.
· Tensing your neck.

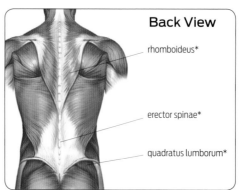

Back View

rhomboideus*

erector spinae*

quadratus lumborum*

3 Gradually roll forward until the roller is beneath your upper back.

4 Roll back to the starting position. Repeat, completing 5 repetitions, and then complete 5 more if desired.

Level
· Intermediate

Duration
· 2–3 minutes

Benefits
· Relieves soreness throughout back
· Improves range of motion

Caution
· Lower-back pain
· Shoulder issues

Annotation Key
* indicates deep muscles

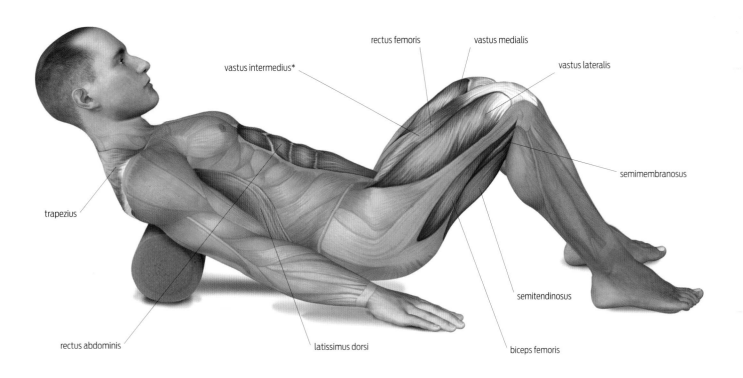

rectus femoris

vastus medialis

vastus lateralis

vastus intermedius*

semimembranosus

trapezius

semitendinosus

rectus abdominis

latissimus dorsi

biceps femoris

Thread the Needle

This exercise focuses on stretching and strengthening the shoulders, abs, and quads through a slow, controlled, back and forward movement. Be aware of the muscles in your shoulders and do not risk straining them to achieve more distance in the movment.

1 Sit upright with your hands on the floor by your sides, palms down. Place the foam roller beneath your knees.

2 Keeping your legs firm, press your hands into the floor as you slowly raise your hips until they are level with your knees.

3 Draw your hips backward through your arms, rolling your legs over the roller. Drop your head slightly so that your gaze is directed toward your thighs.

4 Moving slowly and with control, roll back to the starting position. Keep your hips lifted off the floor. Repeat, aiming for 15 repetitions.

Correct form
· Keep your torso upright and facing forward.
· Keep your abdominal muscles engaged.

Avoid
· Twisting to either side.
· Letting your abs bulge outward.
· Twisting your neck.
· Keep your arms anchored to the floor, as stable as possible.

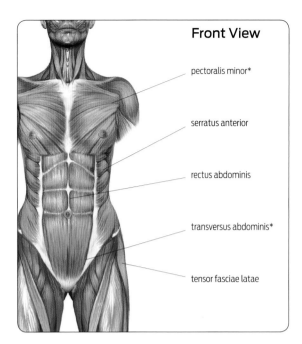

Front View

pectoralis minor*

serratus anterior

rectus abdominis

transversus abdominis*

tensor fasciae latae

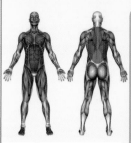

Level
· Intermediate

Duration
· 1–2 minutes

Benefits
· Stabilizes core, pelvis and shoulders
· Strengthens triceps and core muscles

Caution
· Lower-back pain
· Shoulder issues
· Wrist problems

Annotation Key
* indicates deep muscles

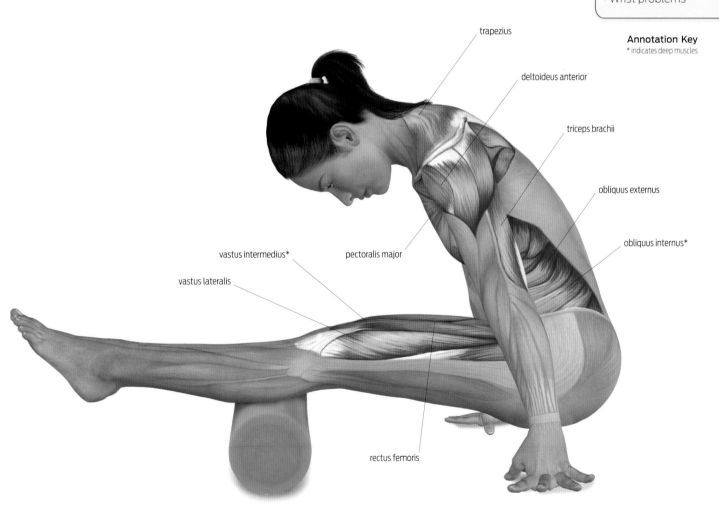

trapezius

deltoideus anterior

triceps brachii

obliquus externus

obliquus internus*

vastus intermedius*

pectoralis major

vastus lateralis

rectus femoris

Contents

Now that you've gained familiarity with the exercises in this book, try putting them together to form combinations that can function within your daily routine. When your alarm goes off at the crack of dawn, but you'd rather just crawl back into bed, start with Body Blitz. And when you're running to catch the train home—maybe shouldering a giant work bag, maybe balancing in high heels—take comfort in the Tension Buster you can complete when the day is done. From head to toe, you'll feel the benefits of these targeted routines.

Workouts

Body Blitz

This challenging workout will give you a burst of energy, burning calories in the process. Keep your pace up as you move through the exercises.

1 Warm-Up Obstacle Course, page 20

2 Figure 8, page 76

5 Knee Raise with Lateral Extension, page 78

4 Lateral-Extension Lateral Lunge, page 72

3 Twisting Knee Raise, page 48

6 Functional Burpee, page 32

7 Mountain Climber, page 34

8 Kneeling Side Lift, page 132

9 Heel Raise with Overhead Press, page 70

10 Obstacle Challenge, page 96

The Core of It

Imagine your navel pressing toward your spine and relax your shoulders and engage your glutes as you feel the powerhouse muscles of your core working, strong and functional.

1 Functional Burpee, page 32

2 Mountain Climber, page 34

5 Swimming, page 52

4 Heel Beat, page 50

3 Seated Russian Twist, page 86

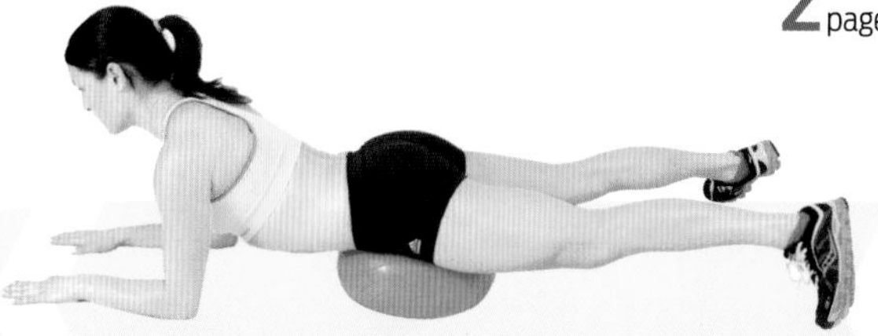

6 Kneeling Side Lift, page 132

7 Push-Up Walkout, page 44

8 Swiss Ball Pullover, page 88

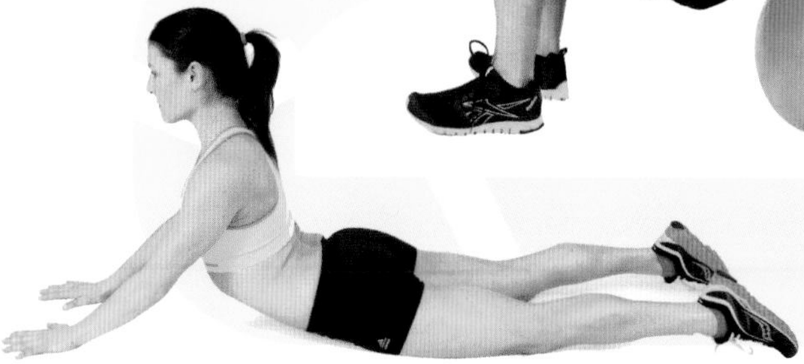

9 Cobra Stretch, page 130

10 Gluteal Roll, page 136

Work-to-Party Toner

This routine will tone your arms and the backs of your legs without wiping you out for the evening. At the end, hold your Iliotibial Band Stretch for an extra 10 seconds and then slowly roll up, vertebra by vertebra.

1 Cobra Stretch, page 130

2 Full-Body Roll, page 60

3 Swiss Ball Bridging Raise, page 56

4 Chin-Up with Hanging Leg Raise, page 58

5 Swimming, page 52

6 Roll-Up Triceps Lift, page 82

7 Gluteal Roll, page 136

8 Latissimus Roll, page 137

9 Supine Hamstrings Stretch, page 126

10 Iliotibial Band Stretch, page 125

Leg Interlude

Practised twice a week, this workout soon cultivates killer legs—an asset whether you're male or female. Bonus: you can do it at your desk.

1 Chair Plié, page 26

2 Chair Squat, page 28

3 Leg-Extension Chair Dip, page 40

4 Diagonal Reach, page 22

5 Lateral-Extension Reverse Lunge, page 24

6 Split Squat with Overhead Press, page 30

7 Pectoral Stretch, page 115

8 Quadriceps Stretch, page 117

9 Triceps Stretch, page 114

10 Calf Stretch, page 116

Postural Pick-Me-Up

This routine works your primary and secondary chest muscles as well as your core and lower back. As much as possible, keep your spine in neutral, neither arched nor hunched forward; when bending over, as in Dead Lift, move smoothly and with control.

1 Twisting Knee Raise, page 48

2 Jumping Lunge, page 36

3 Split Squat with Overhead Press, page 30

4 One-Legged Step-Down, page 42

5 Swiss Ball Pullover, page 88

6 Swiss Ball Jackknife, page 38

7 Dead Lift, page 80

8 Ball Squat with Biceps Curl, page 90

9 Arm-Reach Plank, page 46

10 Heel Beat, page 50

Strengthen & Lengthen

Activated arms and legs plus a pulled-in belly will help you complete this full-body workout. Keep movements controlled, focus on total balance, and stop if you find yourself jerking, slumping, or hunching.

1 Twisting Lift, page 102

2 Hip Extension with Reverse Fly, page 110

3 Clean-and-Press, page 66

4 Lateral-Extension Lateral Lunge, page 72

5 Ball Squat with Biceps Curl, page 90

6 Heel Raise with Overhead Press, page 70

7 Side Adductor Stretch, page 128

8 Pectoral Stretch, page 115

9 Piriformis Stretch, page 118

10 Full-Body Roll, page 60

Back Care Sequence

Your back supports the majority of your functional activities, whether you are swinging a tennis racket or sitting in a driver's seat. Treat it well with these movements, and remember: if an activity causes strain, back off.

2 Diagonal Reach, page 22

1 Full-Body Roll, page 60

3 Squat and Row, page 104

4 Piriformis Bridge, page 54

5 Chin-Up with Hanging Leg Raise, page 58

6 Swimming, page 52

7 Neck Flexion, page 122

8 Latissimus Roll, page 137

9 Cobra Stretch, page 130

10 Back Roll, page 140

Tension Buster

When you sense stress or stiffness in your body, turn to this stretching and releasing workout for relief.

1 Quadriceps Roll, page 134

2 Hamstrings Roll, page 135

4 Latissimus Roll, page 137

5 Tensor Fasciae Latae Roll, page 138

3 Gluteal Roll, page 136

6 Back Roll, page 140

7 Thread the Needle, page 142

8 Neck Flexion, page 122

9 Neck Side Bend, page 123

10 Iliotibial Band Stretch, page 124

Weight-Room Roundup

Remember to work with care
when working with weights: if you
find your form suffering, switch
to a different exercise rather than
adding more and more repetitions.

2 Push-Up Walkout,
page 44

1 Functional Burpee,
page 32

10 Twisting Lift,
page 102

9 Crossover Step-Up,
page 94

11 Lateral-Extension Lateral
Lunge, page 72

12 Knee Raise with Lateral
Extension, page 78

18 Hip-to-Thigh
Stretch, page 120

20 Cobra Stretch,
page 130

19 Triceps Stretch,
page 114

3 Clean-and-Press, page 66

4 Reverse Lunge with Chest Press, page 106

5 Press and Squat, page 108

8 Lateral Step and Curl, page 92

7 Dead Lift, page 80

6 Reach-and-Twist Walking Lunge, page 64

14 Lying Abduction, page 84

13 Woodchop, page 100

17 Knee-Flexion Ball Throw, page 68

16 Roll-Up Triceps Lift, page 82

15 Swiss Ball Pullover, page 88

Body Balancer

This workout will cultivate your sense of balance. Practice it in sequence and keep breathing, inhaling to prepare and exhaling as you execute the moves. Picture yourself growing leaner, stronger, and more centered as you work.

1 Twisting Knee Raise, page 48

2 Reverse Lunge with Chest Press, page 106

8 Leg-Extension Chair Dip, page 40

10 Thread the Needle, page 142

9 One-Legged Step-Down, page 42

18 Cobra Stretch, page 130

17 Calf Stretch, page 116

16 Triceps Stretch, page 114

4 Arm-Reach Plank, page 46

3 Press and Squat, page 108

7 Swiss Ball Jackknife, page 38

6 Kneeling Side Lift, page 132

5 Hip Extension with Reverse Fly, page 110

11 Quadriceps Stretch, page 117

12 Side Adductor Stretch, page 128

13 Tensor Fasciae Latae Roll, page 138

15 Pectoral Stretch, page 115

14 Back Roll, page 140

Glossary

GENERAL TERMINOLOGY
(Note: * indicates deep muscles)

abduction: Movement away from the body.

adduction: Movement toward the body.

anterior: Located in the front.

cardiovascular exercise: Any exercise that increases the heart rate, making available oxygen and nutrient-rich blood to muscles.

cardiovascular system: The circulatory system that distributes blood throughout the body; it includes the heart, lungs, arteries, veins, and capillaries.

core: Refers to the deep muscle layers that lie close to the spine and provide structural support for the entire body. The core is divisible into major core and minor core. The major-core muscles are on the trunk and include the belly area and the mid- and lower back. This area encompasses the pelvic-floor muscles (levator ani, pubococcygeus, iliococcygeus, pubo-rectalis and coccygeus), the abdominals (rectus abdominis, transversus abdominis*, obliquus externus and obliquus internus*), the spinal extensors (multifidus spinae*, erector spinae*, splenius*, longissimus thoracis and semispinalis*) and the diaphragm. The minor core muscles include the latissimus dorsi, gluteus maximus and trapezius (upper, middle and lower). These minor core muscles assist the major muscles when the body engages in activities or movements that require added stability.

crunch: A common abdominal exercise that calls for curling the shoulders toward the pelvis while lying supine with your hands behind the head and your knees bent.

curl: An exercise movement, usually targeting the biceps brachii, that calls for a weight to be moved through an arc, in a "curling" motion.

dead lift: An exercise movement that calls for lifting a weight, such as a barbell, off the ground from a stabilized bent-over position.

dumbbell: A basic piece of equipment that consists of a short bar on which weight plates are secured. A person can use a dumbbell in one or both hands during an exercise. Most gyms offer dumbbells with the weight plates welded on and the number of pounds indicated on the plates, but many dumbbells intended for home use come with removable plates that allow you to adjust the weight.

dynamic exercise: An exercise that includes movement through the joints and muscles.

extension: The act of straightening.

extensor muscle: A muscle serving to extend a body part away from the body.

flexion: The bending of a joint.

flexor muscle: A muscle that decreases the angle between two bones, such as bending the arm at the elbow or raising the thigh toward the stomach.

fly: An exercise movement in which the hand and arm move through an arc while the elbow is kept at a constant angle. A fly works the muscles of the upper body.

iliotibial band (ITB): A thick band of fibrous tissue that runs down the outside of the leg, beginning at the hip and extending to the outer side of the tibia, just below the knee joint. The ITB works in conjunction with several of the thigh muscles to provide stability to the outside of the knee joint.

lateral: Located on, or extending toward, the outside.

medial: Located on, or extending toward, the middle.

medicine ball: A small weighted ball that is used in weight training and toning.

neutral position (spine): A spinal position resembling an S shape, consisting of a lordosis (backward curvature) in the lower back, when viewed in profile.

posterior: Located behind.

press: An exercise movement that calls for moving a weight, or other resistance, away from the body.

range of motion: The distance and direction a joint can move between the flexed position and the extended position.

resistance band: Any rubber tubing or flat band device used for strength training that provides a resistive force. Also called a "fitness band," "stretching band" and "stretch tube".

rotator muscle: One of a group of muscles that assist the rotation of a joint, such as the hip or the shoulder.

scapula: The "shoulder blade," a protrusion of bone on the mid- to upper back.

squat: An exercise that calls for moving the hips back and bending the knees and hips to lower the torso (and an accompanying weight, if desired) and then returning to the upright position. A squat primarily targets the muscles of the thighs, hips, and buttocks, as well as the hamstrings.

static exercise: An isometric form of exercise, without movement of the joints, where a position is held for a specific period of time.

Swiss ball: A flexible, inflatable PVC ball, 14–34 inches in circumference, used for weight training, physical therapy, balance training and other exercise regimens. It is also called a "balance ball," "fitness ball," "stability ball," "exercise ball," "gym ball," "physioball," "body ball," and many other names.

warm-up: Any light exercise of short duration that prepares the body for mor- intense activity.

weight: Refers to the plates or weight stacks, or the actual poundage listed on the bar or dumbbell.

LATIN TERMINOLOGY

The following glossary explains the Latin terminology used to describe the body's musculature. Where words are derived from the Greek, this is indicated.

Chest

coracobrachialis: Greek *korakoeidés*, "ravenlike," and *brachium*, "arm"

pectoralis (major and minor): *pectus*, "breast"

Abdomen

obliquus externus: *obliquus*, "slanting," and *externus*, "outwards"

obliquus internus: *obliquus*, "slanting," and *internus*, "within"

rectus abdominis: *rego*, "straight, upright," and *abdomen*, "belly"

serratus anterior: *serra*, "saw," and *ante*, "before"

transversus abdominis: *transversus*, "athwart, across," and *abdomen*, "belly"

Neck

scalenus: Greek *skalénós*, "unequal"

semispinalis: *semi*, "half," and *spinae*, "spine"

splenius: Greek *splénion*, "plaster, patch"

sternocleidomastoideus: Greek *stérnon*, "chest," Greek *kleís*, "key," and Greek *mastoeidés*, "breastlike"

Back

erector spinae: *erectus*, "straight," and *spinae*, "spine"

latissimus dorsi: *latus*, "wide," and *dorsum*, "back"

multifidus spinae: *multifid*, "to cut into divisions," and *spinae*, "spine"

quadratus lumborum: *quadratus*, "square, rectangular," and *lumbus*, "loin"

rhomboideus: Greek *rhembesthai*, "to spin"

trapezius: Greek *trapezion*, "small table"

Shoulders

deltoideus anterior: Greek *deltoeidés*, "delta-shaped" (that is, triangular), and *ante*, "before"

deltoideus medialis: Greek *deltoeidés*, "delta-shaped" (that is, triangular), and *medialis*, "middle"

deltoideus posterior: Greek *deltoeidés*, "delta-shaped" (that is, triangular), and *posterus*, "behind"

infraspinatus: *infra*, "under," and *spinae*, "spine"

levator scapulae: *levare*, "to raise," and *scapulae*, "shoulder [blades]"

subscapularis: *sub*, "below," and *scapulae*, "shoulder [blades]"

supraspinatus: *supra*, "above," and *spinae*, "spine"

teres (major and minor): *teres*, "rounded"

Upper Arm

biceps brachii: *biceps*, "two-headed," and *brachium*, "arm"

brachialis: *brachium*, "arm"

triceps brachii: *triceps*, "three-headed," and *brachium*, "arm"

Lower Arm

anconeus: Greek *anconad*, "elbow"

brachioradialis: *brachium*, "arm," and *radius*, "spoke"

extensor carpi radialis: *extendere*, "to extend," Greek *karpós*, "wrist," and *radius*, "spoke"

extensor digitorum: *extendere*, "to extend," and *digitus*, "finger, toe"

flexor carpi pollicis longus: *flectere*, "to bend," Greek *karpós*, "wrist," *pollicis*, "thumb," and *longus*, "long"

flexor carpi radialis: *flectere*, "to bend," Greek *karpós*, "wrist," and *radius*, "spoke"

flexor carpi ulnaris: *flectere*, "to bend," Greek *karpós*, "wrist," and *ulnaris*, "forearm"

flexor digitorum: *flectere*, "to bend," and *digitus*, "finger, toe"

palmaris longus: *palmaris*, "palm," and *longus*, "long"

pronator teres: *pronate*, "to rotate," and *teres*, "rounded"

Hips

gemellus: *geminus*, "twin"

gluteus maximus: Greek *gloutós*, "rump," and *maximus*, "largest"

gluteus medius: Greek *gloutós*, "rump," and *medialis*, "middle"

gluteus minimus: Greek *gloutós*, "rump," and *minimus*, "smallest"

iliacus: *ilium*, "groin"

iliopsoas: *ilium*, "groin," and Greek *psoa*, "groin muscle"

obturator externus: *obturare*, "to block," and *externus*, "outward"

obturator internus: *obturare*, "to block," and *internus*, "within"

pectineus: *pectin*, "comb"

piriformis: *pirum*, "pear," and *forma*, "shape"

quadratus femoris: *quadratus*, "square, rectangular," and *femur*, "thigh"

Upper Leg

adductor longus: *adducere*, "to contract," and *longus*, "long"

adductor magnus: *adducere*, "to contract," and *magnus*, "major"

biceps femoris: *biceps*, "two-headed," and *femur*, "thigh"

gracilis: *gracilis*, "slim, slender"

rectus femoris: *rego*, "straight, upright," and *femur*, "thigh"

sartorius: *sarcio*, "to patch, to repair"

semimembranosus: *semi*, "half," and *membrum*, "limb"

semitendinosus: *semi*, "half," and *tendo*, "tendon"

tensor fasciae latae: *tendere*, "to stretch," *fasciae*, "band," and *latae*, "laid down"

vastus intermedius: *vastus*, "immense, huge," and *intermedius*, "between"

vastus lateralis: *vastus*, "immense, huge," and *lateralis*, "side"

vastus medialis: *vastus*, "immense, huge," and *medialis*, "middle"

Lower Leg

adductor digiti minimi: *adducere*, "to contract," *digitus*, "finger, toe," and *minimum* "smallest"

adductor hallucis: *adducere*, "to contract," and *hallex*, "big toe"

extensor digitorum: *extendere*, "to extend," and *digitus*, "finger, toe"

extensor hallucis: *extendere*, "to extend," and *hallex*, "big toe"

flexor digitorum: *flectere*, "to bend," and *digitus*, "finger, toe"

flexor hallucis: *flectere*, "to bend," and *hallex*, "big toe"

gastrocnemius: Greek *gastroknémía*, "calf [of the leg]"

peroneus: *peronei*, "of the *fibula*"

plantaris: *planta*, "sole"

soleus: *solea*, "sandal"

tibialis anterior: *tibia*, "reed pipe," and *ante*, "before"

tibialis posterior: *tibia*, "reed pipe," and *posterus*, "behind"

trochlea tali: *trochleae*, "pulley-shaped structure," and *talus*, "lower portion of ankle joint"

About the Authors

Erica Gordon-Mallin

Growing up, Erica Gordon-Mallin would have chosen the library over the gym any day. But now, as a writer and seasoned fitness book editor, she is delighted to have found functional training, with its focus on how we move our whole bodies in real life. She finds the results wonderfully effective, and intends to follow this fitness approach for many years to come. A graduate of Amherst College and University College London, Erica lives in Manhattan.

Erica's Acknowledgments

A big thank you to Lisa Purcell, whose work in developing this series laid the groundwork for *Anatomy of Functional Training* and so many other fitness books still to come. Big thanks also to Hollis Liebman who advised on the muscle diagrams, coming through with flying colours on short notice. Thank you to Danielle Scaramuzzo for her early design work. And on a personal note, I would like to thank my always-supportive father, Sam Mallin; my grammar inspiration, Marion Wolfthal; and Mariel Gold, my sister and best friend.

Katerina Spilio

At the age of 16, Katerina Spilio began climbing on scaffolding to decorate church ceilings with her father. The need for strength, flexibility, and endurance became quickly apparent and led to a lifelong fitness career. As a personal trainer certified by the Aerobics and Fitness Association of America, for over 30 years she has taught countless group classes and individual sessions—including at Rye Personal Fitness and Mind and Body Fitness in New York. A firm believer in the mind—body connection, she continues to motivate and train people in functional exercise, while also maintaining her ecclesiastic artwork studio in Dobbs Ferry, New York

Katerina's Acknowledgments

I would like to thank my father, the late Reverend John Spilio who taught me to exercise every day of my life, and my mother Mary, ever svelte and fit, who provides an incredible role model. Thanks also to my daughters Ariadne and Alexandra for whom I always strive to be a better person.

Credits

Photography

Photography by FineArtsPhotoGroup.com
Models: Joseph Benedict, Jillian Langenau

Illustrations

All large illustrations by Hector Aiza/3D Labz Animation India, except the insets throughout and the full-body anatomy art works on pages 16 and 17: by Linda Bucklin/Shutterstock.

Acknowledgments

The author and publisher also offer thanks to those closely involved in the creation of this book: Moseley Road President Sean Moore, General Manager Karen Prince, art director Tina Vaughan, production director Adam Moore, editor Jo Weeks; and designer Heather McCarry.